Robert C. Elliott, the editor of this
volume in the *Twentieth Century Inter-*
pretations series, is Professor of English
Literature and Chairman of the Depart-
ment of Literature at the University of
California, San Diego. He is the author of
The Power of Satire and *The Shape of*
Utopia.

TWENTIETH CENTURY INTERPRETATIONS
OF

MOLL FLANDERS

TWENTIETH CENTURY INTERPRETATIONS
OF

MOLL FLANDERS

A Collection of Critical Essays

Edited by
ROBERT C. ELLIOTT

Prentice-Hall, Inc. A SPECTRUM BOOK *Englewood Cliffs, N. J.*

Contents

v

Acknowledgments

I would like to thank Andrew Wright and Jan Altizer for help in preparing this volume.

TWENTIETH CENTURY INTERPRETATIONS
OF

MOLL FLANDERS

Introduction

by Robert C. Elliott

Alexander Pope put Defoe in the *Dunciad;* Swift, when he could remember Defoe's name, scorned him as a "grave, sententious, dogmatical . . . rogue," who was beyond enduring; and the professionally mild Joseph Addison, exploding into fury at Defoe's political shenanigans, called him "a false, shuffling, prevaricating rascal." In the cant terms of our time, Pope, Swift, and Addison were members of the Establishment attacking an outsider. For almost forty years Defoe struggled with incredible persistence to "make it"; but although he was a popular writer, the Establishment was always well beyond his reach. History, however, has redeemed him. At least fifteen of Defoe's most important works are currently in print, including the nine-volume *Review*. In the last few years he has been the subject of half a dozen book-length studies and many learned articles. The present volume is the second in the Twentieth Century Interpretations series to be devoted to a work of Defoe—the first, on *Robinson Crusoe*, edited by Frank Ellis, appeared in 1969. Defoe is read, studied, argued over, enjoyed. If the Establishment was beyond him in his own day, he has certainly made it now.

Daniel Defoe (1660–1731) was born an outsider. His father, James Foe, a London chandler, bred him for the Dissenting ministry. "It was my disaster," Defoe wrote in retrospect, "first to be set apart for, and then to be set apart from, the honour of that sacred employ." He was seduced by his love of trade, "the whore I doated on," he said; and early in life he plunged into business with the incredible energy that was to mark everything he did. His career was spectacularly spotty: a good marriage, early success and prosperity, the addition of "De" to his name in a bid for gentility, speculative losses, a series of lawsuits accusing him of various kinds of chicanery, his swindling of his own mother-in-law, and then, in 1692, a thumping bankruptcy to the tune of £17,000. Terrified at the prospect of debtor's prison, Defoe fled, the first of many times that he would go underground to avoid the importunities of creditors and the law.

His career as a merchant in ruins, Defoe turned to writing to make a living, commerce's loss becoming literature's gain—although much of what Defoe wrote in an unprecedentedly prolific career can be called literature by courtesy only. We know him as a novelist; but he was pamphleteer, journalist, party hack, poet: writer on projects and trade, economics and religion, travel, manners, education, courtship, ghosts, pirates, plagues . . . even voyages to the moon. What subject did he not touch? A politically unprincipled man, Defoe worked for years as secret political agent for Robert Harley, Tory Prime Minister under Queen Anne; then when Harley fell from office, Defoe turned around and did the same for the Whigs, writing with full eloquence and seeming conviction on both sides of touchy political issues. It was a risky life; and, not surprisingly, his genuine convictions got him into trouble. Defoe remained true to the Dissenting faith he had been born to. He was violently opposed to the practice of "occasional conformity," according to which Dissenters qualified themselves for public office by occasionally taking communion in the Anglican church. This, said Defoe, "was *playing Bo-peep* with God Almighty." Attacks on the Dissenters from High Church extremists multiplied in the early years of Queen Anne's reign. In 1702 Defoe issued an ironic pamphlet, *The Shortest Way with the Dissenters,* in which he impersonated an Anglican zealot who pushed ideas being bandied about to absurd lengths:

> 'Tis vain to trifle in this matter. The light, foolish handling of them by Mulcts, Fines etc., 'tis their Glory and their Advantage. If the Gallows instead of the Counter, and the Gallies instead of the Fines, were the Reward of going to a Conventicle, to preach or hear, there wou'd not be so many sufferers.

It was as though a draft resister today should write an article, ironically recommending that anyone listening to Dr. Spock or Noam Chomsky be thrown into a concentration camp. In a time of hysteria Defoe's irony worked too well and the pamphlet was read literally. Anglican extremists thought it "a brat of their own begetting" and welcomed the wild proposals; Dissenters were thoroughly frightened. Defoe fled to avoid arrest; but after several months he was taken, sentenced to stand in the pillory, and then thrown into Newgate prison. The horror of Newgate, expressed so vividly in *Moll Flanders,* was honestly earned.

Defoe's great literary triumph, of course, was *Robinson Crusoe* (1719), written when he was sixty years old. The success of that book begot other long narratives, produced in a torrent of creative energy to which there seemed no limit. In 1722 alone he published *Moll Flanders, Due Preparations for the Plague, A Journal of the Plague Year,* and *Colonel Jacque,* to say nothing of an instructional dialogue called *Religious Courtship* and assorted pamphlets and newspaper

pieces. What combination of compulsions lay behind such phenom-
enal activity, it is, of course, impossible to say, although one motivat-
ing force can be isolated with assurance. Throughout his career Defoe
was driven by a desire to be able to live the life he tirelessly celebrated
in his work—that of middle-class gentility.[1] For short periods he had
his wish, but Defoe was born under an unlucky star and he ended
his life as he had begun it, an outsider. Defoe's last months were
spent in hiding from one of the creditors who eternally hounded him.
Moll Flanders, whose ambitions were those of her author, had better
luck.

Fifty years ago a distinguished scholar found the full title of *Moll
Flanders* unprintable, so scandalous were the allurements it advertised:

THE FORTUNES AND MISFORTUNES OF THE FAMOUS

Moll Flanders &c.

*Who was Born in Newgate, and during a Life of continu'd
Variety for Threescore Years, besides her Childhood, was
Twelve Year a Whore, five times a Wife (whereof once to
her own Brother), Twelve Year a Thief, Eight Year a
Transported Felon in Virginia, at last grew Rich, liv'd
Honest, and died a Penitent, Written from her own
Memorandums . . .*

Readers of our day will not be surprised that attacks on the book on
moral grounds did nothing to diminish its popularity. Three editions
were called for in 1722, the year *Moll Flanders* was published, and a
fourth in the year following. In 1728 John Gay's *The Beggar's Opera*,
which also had thieves and whores as central characters, had a parallel
success, and it too was roundly damned by moralists. Sir John Fielding
tried to have the play banned, largely on the grounds that it was
responsible for a spectacular increase in the number of highway
robberies being committed in emulation of the dashing Macheath.
According to Boswell, Edward Gibbon, the historian, thought the
pernicious effects of *The Beggar's Opera* more than offset by the
civilizing influence it exerted on robbers, "making them less ferocious,
more polite, in short, more like gentlemen." There is no evidence
that *Moll Flanders* had a comparable effect on the whores of London,
although if any of them had read the book, and taken its lessons to
heart, there might well have been a marked rise in the level of gentility
in that profession.

[1] Michael Shinagel, *Daniel Defoe and Middle-Class Gentility* (Cambridge: Harvard
University Press, 1968) provides full documentation.

The Beggar's Opera could easily have accommodated a number of characters from Defoe's novel. If Macheath was "one of God Almighty's gentlemen," as Macaulay was to call him, so was Jemmy, Moll's Lancashire husband, who could have moved into Gay's cast of characters with no trouble at all. So could some of Moll's anonymous cohorts in the trade: "I knew a woman," writes Moll, "that was so dextrous with a fellow . . . that, while he was busie with her in another way, convey'd his purse with twenty guineas in it out of his fob pocket, where he had put it for fear of her" (p. 198).[2] At a gathering of the whores in *The Beggar's Opera* Jenny Diver is praised for the same dexterity: "Though her fellow be never so agreeable, she can pick his pocket as cooly, as if money were her only pleasure. Now that is a command of the passions uncommon in a woman!" The tone of the two passages is oddly similar, although Moll's ill-concealed admiration is that of a craftsman for a true master, whereas the comment on Jenny has the cynicism of a Lord Rochester. But the two works actually have little besides milieu in common. *The Beggar's Opera* is Augustan in its aristocratic wit, its firm control of style, its precise and pointed satire. Despite Dr. Johnson's claim that Gay's comedy was written only to divert and had no moral purpose whatever, the work is infused with the kind of moral thrust that satire purports to exert. As Gay's friend Jonathan Swift said, defending *The Beggar's Opera* against charges of immorality, satire laughs men out of their follies and vices. We snort at Peachum's, "My daughter to me should be, like a court lady to a minister of state, a key to the whole gang"; or at Polly's, "A woman knows how to be mercenary, though she hath never been in a court or at an assembly"; and then we make the identifications enforced by the entire play: the moral life of courtiers and ministers of state is indistinguishable from that of the Newgate birds. Gay's satirical purpose is evident enough.

Matters are by no means so clear in *Moll Flanders*. In his Preface Defoe claims to be presenting the story of a wicked life crowned by repentance and success. Readers, he trusts, will be *"more pleas'd with the moral than the fable, with the application than with the relation, and with the end of the writer than with the life of the person written of"* (p. 4). It is characteristic of Defoe that there should be some ambiguity about who "the writer" is whose end we are to attend to— Defoe or Moll. Their purposes and points of view are often very hard to disentangle, to the confusion of the reader; for Moll, whether penitent or not, is a dubious guide to the virtuous life. As a writer of her own memoirs, she is marvelously adept at controlling our sym-

---

[2] Quotations from *Moll Flanders* are from the edition by James Sutherland (Boston: Houghton Mifflin Company, 1959). Page numbers are given in parentheses in the text.

pathies. We want her to get away with the gold watch and the yards of Flanders lace, with the horse that she almost absentmindedly purloins; and we are likely to listen sympathetically as she deplores the wickedness of her actions while planning the next day's foray. This is human nature, we think. Moll's repentances, like most of our own, are skin-deep, to be taken seriously only until the next temptation presents itself. Defoe, if not Moll, understands these things. But then an episode or even a phrase throws us into doubt. For example, while she is imprisoned in Newgate, Moll hears that three highwaymen— "brave, topping gentlemen"—have been captured, "after a gallant resistance, in which many of the country people were wounded, and some kill'd" (p. 244). The whole tone of the passage enlists our sympathies for the outlaws, just as in the movies we are seduced into exulting as the "bad" guys in a Western hold up a bank, or as Bonnie and Clyde shoot their way out of a trap. In *Moll Flanders* as in the movies, "the country people . . . killed" have little weight in the moral balance. It is a nice problem for the reader to work out how, writing after her sincere repentance, Moll stands in relation to the phrase "gallant resistance," to say nothing of how Defoe stands.

Or again, Moll recounts how her governess tries to bribe the two wenches who caught Moll in the theft that sent her to Newgate. The first girl, whose wages are £3 a year, turns down a bribe of £100 in order to testify against Moll. Years after the event, penitent or no, Moll is still furious at the "hard mouth'd jades" who convicted her, although she is forced to admit that their testimony was accurate. Her account of the trial (p. 248) is a swirl of psychological and moral confusions, a paradigm of what Howard Koonce calls, in one of the essays in this volume, "Moll's muddle." Dr. Johnson claimed that in *The Beggar's Opera* there is "such a *labefaction* of all principles as may be injurious to morality." But in Gay's play the principles are there, transvalued though they may be, and we know how to make the appropriate corrections. There is a great deal of talk about morality in *Moll Flanders*, but labefaction arises from muddle.

The question as to whose muddle it is—Moll's or Defoe's—has occupied critics and historians for a good many years as they have tried to place Defoe in the tradition of the English novel. F. R. Leavis, in 1945, contemptuously dismissed earlier claims made by Virginia Woolf and E. M. Forster that *Moll Flanders* was a great novel; not deigning to document his case, he referred readers, for all that need be said, to an essay on Defoe by Leslie Stephen, Virginia Woolf's father.[3] Stephen had been markedly unsympathetic. Defoe's great

---

[3] Leslie Stephen, "Defoe's Novels," in *Hours in a Library* (New York, 1892), I, 1–46.

power for giving verisimilitude to his fictions resulted, he said, simply
from the fact that Defoe had "the most amazing talent on record for
telling lies." Unhappily, said Stephen, Defoe was not aware of the
distinction between the art of lying and the art of fiction. *Moll Flanders*, verisimilitude and all, has no more interest than a detailed police
report. Stephen could not have known of the twentieth-century taste
for the police-court style: the "scrupulous accumulation of details,"
which police reports aspire to, constitutes the lifeblood of the novel,
says Norman Mailer. Still it is surprising to find Virginia Woolf, who
had no love for circumstantiality of report, praising *Moll Flanders*
in the enthusiastic terms she used: one of the "few English novels which
we can call indisputably great," she writes in the essay included in this
volume. It is less surprising to find critics who have a Marxist orientation concurring in her evaluation.[4] From their point of view, *Moll
Flanders* can be looked upon as a "proletarian" work, with Moll as
society's victim: "the human relation becomes a property relation,
and it is the woman who suffers. That is the theme of *Moll Flanders*."
So writes Alick West, who has the highest praise for Defoe's insight
into sociological relations, his feeling for the "restless energy of hu-
manity."

If John Peale Bishop can find *Moll Flanders* "perhaps the greatest
of English novels," critics who concentrate on the "muddle" referred
to above question whether it is really a novel at all. Mark Schorer
thinks that it is not. In his view a necessary condition of the novel is
that its materials must be judged in ways that were not available to
Daniel Defoe:

> At the end we discover that Moll turns virtuous only after a life of
> vice has enabled her to do so with security. The actualities of the book,
> then, enforce the moral assumption of any commercial culture, the belief
> that virtue and worldly goods form an equation . . . . [This is] the
> morality of measurement, and without in the least intending it, *Moll
> Flanders* is our classic revelation of the mercantile mind: the morality of
> measurement which Defoe has apparently neglected to measure.[5]

Ian Watt, in a detailed, circumstantial, very powerful essay—only
part of which can be included here—arrived at conclusions similar to
those of Schorer, particularly on the question of Defoe's command, or
lack thereof, over his materials. The issue is basically whether or not

---

[4] See John Peale Bishop, "Moll Flanders' Way," in *Collected Essays*, ed. Edmund
Wilson (New York and London: Charles Scribner's Sons, 1948), pp. 47–55; Alick West,
The Mountain in the Sunlight (London: Lawrence and Wishart, 1958), pp. 59–109;
Arnold Kettle, "In Defence of *Moll Flanders*," in *Of Books and Humankind*, ed.
John Butt (London: Routledge & Kegan Paul, Ltd., 1964), pp. 55–67.

[5] Mark Schorer, Introduction to the Modern Library College Edition of *Moll
Flanders* (1950).

there is an ironic remove, in any large sense, between Moll and her creator. As against Virginia Woolf's praise of the design in Defoe's novels, Watt finds no structural control whatever. There are, he concedes, local examples of conscious irony, as when little Moll prophetically declares that when she grows up she will be a gentlewoman like the town whore who does not do housework and is called "madam." Instead of forming part of a comprehensive pattern, however, most of the ironic passages, Watt maintains, are properly to be regarded as accidents, "produced by the random application of narrative authenticity to conflicts in Defoe's social and moral and religious world, accidents which unwittingly reveal to us the serious discrepancies in his system of values. . . . *Moll Flanders* is undoubtedly an ironic object, but it is not a work of irony."

Influential as Watt's essay has been, it has come under sharp attack.[6] Dorothy Van Ghent concedes that the morality preached by Moll and substantiated by the Author's Preface is a burlesque of genuine morality, but argues that it is a burlesque contained and ordered by the ironic structure of the work. We are faced by two possibilities, she says: "Either *Moll Flanders* is a collection of scandal-sheet anecdotes naively patched together with the platitudes that form the morality of an impoverished soul (Defoe's), a 'sincere' soul but a confused and degraded one; or *Moll Flanders* is a great novel, coherent in structure, unified and given its shape and significance by a complex system of ironies." Van Ghent waives the question of Defoe's "intention." The book yields itself, whether by intention or not, to ironic analysis; its greatness is authenticated by the fact that we read and reread it, and we marvel. "We might guess that a great book could not be written by an impoverished soul. . . ."

Maximillian E. Novak (whose *Economics and the Fiction of Defoe* and *Defoe and the Nature of Man* have contributed substantially to our understanding of Defoe's modes of thought) endorses Van Ghent's thesis and lists a series of themes or topics in the novel in the treatment of which Defoe deliberately exercises irony. Arnold Kettle and Howard L. Koonce, in essays mentioned earlier, both undertake refutations of Watt's position, Kettle emphasizing the social dimension of the novel, and Koonce pointing to Defoe's manipulation of Moll's evident confusions:

On the one hand, we have a character compelled towards self-realization and able to act in a series of situations where real spiritual and moral awareness would be paralyzing. And on the other, we have that charac-

[6] In the preparation of this book I have been much indebted to Watt's own "The Recent Critical Fortunes of *Moll Flanders*," *Eighteenth-Century Studies*, I (1967), 109–26.

ter's compulsion towards a moral and spiritual respectability which needs
that awareness to be valid. It is the juxtaposition of these two forces that
creates the real and sustaining conflict of the piece.

The Italian critic Cesare Pavese also finds that the intermingling and
fusing of the extreme motives driving Moll—those of conscience and
of cash—provide the work with a structural irony.

Irony, of course, is not the only perspective from which, in our structural age, the crucial matter of literary morphology can be approached.
Robert Alter, for example, examines the frequently made claims that
Moll Flanders is a picaresque novel, its somewhat haphazard organization sanctioned by the conventions of the genre. Alter advances good
reasons for rejecting those claims. While reading his essay I thought
of a simple—a too simple—test. At the end of his autobiography
Lazarillo de Tormes, the archetypal picaro, records that he achieved
his relative affluence when he married the whore of a priest, an
affluence that he maintains by being cuckolded daily. This is the
period of his life, he says, at which "I had entered into my prosperity
and had attained the summit of all good fortune." [7] The remark
illuminates with a Swiftian harshness the relationship of the picaro
to his world. Moll Flanders, in comparably scandalous circumstances,
says something similar. She has just been delivered of a bastard child
fathered by her Bath lover, and has been installed in handsome lodg-
ings in Hammersmith: "And now I was indeed in the height of what
I might call my prosperity, and I wanted nothing but to be a wife . . ."
(p. 103). If there is a hint of reservation in "what I might call," it is
quickly lost in Moll's calculations about the prudent conduct necessary
to maintain good relations with the man one is being kept by. The
tone of the two comments—so similar in content, so different in
significance—measures the distance between the picaro's world and
Moll's.

Another effort to find structural coherence in *Moll Flanders* is that
of G. A. Starr, who in his book *Defoe and Spiritual Autobiography* shows how spiritual decay and hardening in Moll's career, her
pseudorepentances leading ultimately to a true repentance, provide
an internal organizing principle of the narrative. In a later essay,
hitherto unpublished, Mr. Starr attempts to account for the complexity of our response to Moll by examining closely her skill as a
casuist.

Finally, Lee Edwards, in an essay published here for the first time,
mediates between those who think that Defoe blundered into writing
a great book and those who eulogize him as a master of structure:

[7] *The Life of Lazarillo de Tormes,* trans. W. S. Merwin (New York: Anchor Books,
1964), p. 152.

Crudely put, Defoe's dilemma in *Moll Flanders* has been to find a *modus vivendi* for a poor, solitary girl. The book itself provides evidence for two possible solutions to this problem, the Christian and the secular. In terms of the Christian solution, Moll is made to turn to God. Having found him, she is no longer alone and the things of this world no longer have any great significance. This view is the one voiced by Moll in Newgate and at various other times during the course of the book. In terms of the secular solution, Moll makes both money and marriages. . . . The narrative structure in terms of which both these solutions are worked out is superficially similar: both are circular in form—in my beginning is my end—and spiral in movement. The obvious and unreconciled question, however, concerns the congruence of the two spirals. There are roads to both God and Mammon, but neither the gods nor the roads are necessarily the same.

The debate conducted in the essays that follow is learned, ingenious, sometimes heated, often witty. It involves a major aesthetic issue: the grounds on which critics attempt to establish the literary status of an immensely popular work of fiction. Whatever the disagreements (which, given the scandalous state of our profession, readers are necessarily invited to resolve for themselves), the enduring appeal of the book remains something to conjure with. On one thing all would agree: the appeal is inextricably involved with the character of Moll herself, a woman so full of the life force as to dwarf all around her. Let E. M. Forster have the last word: "She fills the book that bears her name, or rather stands alone in it, like a tree in a park. . . ." [8]

[8] E. M. Forster, *Aspects of the Novel* (New York: Harcourt, Brace, 1954; first published 1927), p. 88.

Moll Flanders

by Reed Whittemore

The story of Flanders, Moll, her fall, is moral.
Hardly nothing is evil done unseen
And slips away for good, but sin is final,
Booked and indexed for a shyster's spleen.

Hell is almost bound by Newgate's wall,
And from within the cry of chastened crime
Breaks on the acting thief to tell
How watches stolen steal the stealing time.

Moll is caught, convicted, and released
A penitent. And thus the Arch Fiend, foiled,
Convinced of his fallacious drift, debased,
Goes back to where he came from spoiled,

To Newgate, where the adamantine doors
Stand open for the felons and the whores.

"Moll Flanders." From Heroes and Heroines *by Reed Whittemore (New York: Reynal and Hitchcock, 1946), p. 47. Copyright 1946 by Reed Whittemore. Reprinted by permission of the author.*

Defoe

by Virginia Woolf

The fear which attacks the recorder of centenaries lest he should find himself measuring a diminishing spectre and forced to foretell its approaching dissolution is not only absent in the case of *Robinson Crusoe* but the mere thought of it is ridiculous. It may be true that *Robinson Crusoe* is two hundred years of age upon the twenty-fifth of April 1919, but far from raising the familiar speculations as to whether people now read it and will continue to read it, the effect of the bicentenary is to make us marvel that *Robinson Crusoe*, the perennial and immortal, should have been in existence so short a time as that. The book resembles one of the anonymous productions of the race rather than the effort of a single mind; and as for celebrating its centenary we should as soon think of celebrating the centenaries of Stonehenge itself. Something of this we may attribute to the fact that we have all had *Robinson Crusoe* read aloud to us as children, and were thus much in the same state of mind towards Defoe and his story that the Greeks were in towards Homer. It never occurred to us that there was such a person as Defoe, and to have been told that *Robinson Crusoe* was the work of a man with a pen in his hand would either have disturbed us unpleasantly or meant nothing at all. The impressions of childhood are those that last longest and cut deepest. It still seems that the name of Daniel Defoe has no right to appear upon the title-page of *Robinson Crusoe*, and if we celebrate the bicentenary of the book we are making a slightly unnecessary allusion to the fact that, like Stonehenge, it is still in existence.

The great fame of the book has done its author some injustice; for while it has given him a kind of anonymous glory it has obscured the fact that he was a writer of other works which, it is safe to assert, were not read aloud to us as children. Thus when the Editor of the *Christian World* in the year 1870 appealed to "the boys and girls of

"Defoe." From The Common Reader *by Virginia Woolf (London: Hogarth Press, Ltd.; New York: Harcourt, Brace & World, Inc., 1933), pp. 121–31. Copyright 1925 by Harcourt, Brace & World, Inc.; copyright 1953 by Virginia Woolf. Reprinted by permission of Quentin Bell, Angelica Garnett, and the publishers.*

England" to erect a monument upon the grave of Defoe, which a stroke of lightning had mutilated, the marble was inscribed to the memory of the author of *Robinson Crusoe*. No mention was made of *Moll Flanders*. Considering the topics which are dealt with in that book, and in *Roxana, Captain Singleton, Colonel Jack* and the rest, we need not be surprised, though we may be indignant, at the omission. We may agree with Mr. Wright, the biographer of Defoe, that these "are not works for the drawing-room table." But unless we consent to make that useful piece of furniture the final arbiter of taste, we must deplore the fact that their superficial coarseness, or the universal celebrity of *Robinson Crusoe*, has led them to be far less widely famed than they deserve. On any monument worthy of the name of monument the names of *Moll Flanders* and *Roxana*, at least, should be carved as deeply as the name of Defoe. They stand among the few English novels which we can call indisputably great. The occasion of the bicentenary of their more famous companion may well lead us to consider in what their greatness, which has so much in common with his, may be found to consist.

Defoe was an elderly man when he turned novelist, many years the predecessor of Richardson and Fielding, and one of the first indeed to shape the novel and launch it on its way. But it is unnecessary to labour the fact of his precedence, except that he came to his novel-writing with certain conceptions about the art which he derived partly from being himself one of the first to practise it. The novel had to justify its existence by telling a true story and preaching a sound moral. "This supplying a story by invention is certainly a most scandalous crime," he wrote. "It is a sort of lying that makes a great hole in the heart, in which by degrees a habit of lying enters in." Either in the preface or in the text of each of his works, therefore, he takes pains to insist that he has not used his invention at all but has depended upon facts, and that his purpose has been the highly moral desire to convert the vicious or to warn the innocent. Happily these were principles that tallied very well with his natural disposition and endowments. Facts had been drilled into him by sixty years of varying fortunes before he turned his experience to account in fiction. "I have some time ago summed up the Scenes of my life in this distich," he wrote:

> No man has tasted differing fortunes more,
> And thirteen times I have been rich and poor.

He had spent eighteen months in Newgate and talked with thieves, pirates, highwaymen, and coiners before he wrote the history of Moll Flanders. But to have facts thrust upon you by dint of living and accident is one thing; to swallow them voraciously and retain the imprint of them indelibly, is another. It is not merely that Defoe knew the stress of poverty and had talked with the victims of it, but that the unsheltered life, exposed to circumstances and forced to shift for itself, appealed to him imaginatively as the right matter for his art. In the first pages of each of his great novels he reduces his hero or heroine to such a state of unfriended misery that their existence must be a continued struggle, and their survival at all the result of luck and their own exertions. Moll Flanders was born in Newgate of a criminal mother; Captain Singleton was stolen as a child and sold to the gipsies; Colonel Jack, though "born a gentleman, was put 'prentice to a pickpocket"; Roxana starts under better auspices, but, having married at fifteen, she sees her husband go bankrupt and is left with five children in "a condition the most deplorable that words can express."

Thus each of these boys and girls has the world to begin and the battle to fight for himself. The situation thus created was entirely to Defoe's liking. From her very birth or with half a year's respite at most, Moll Flanders, the most notable of them, is goaded by "that worst of devils, poverty," forced to earn her living as soon as she can sew, driven from place to place, making no demands upon her creator for the subtle domestic atmosphere which he was unable to supply, but drawing upon him for all he knew of strange people and customs. From the outset the burden of proving her right to exist is laid upon her. She has to depend entirely upon her own wits and judgement, and to deal with each emergency as it arises by a rule-of-thumb morality which she has forged in her own head. The briskness of the story is due partly to the fact that having transgressed the accepted laws at a very early age she has henceforth the freedom of the outcast. The one impossible event is that she should settle down in comfort and security. But from the first the peculiar genius of the author asserts itself, and avoids the obvious danger of the novel of adventure. He makes us understand that Moll Flanders was a woman on her own account and not only material for a succession of adventures. In proof of this she begins, as Roxana also begins, by falling passionately, if unfortunately, in love. That she must rouse herself and marry some one else and look very closely to her settlements and prospects is no slight upon her passion, but to be laid to the charge of her birth; and, like all Defoe's women, she is a person of robust understanding. Since she makes no scruple of telling lies when they serve her purpose, there is something undeniable about her truth when she speaks it. She has no time to waste upon the refinements of personal affection; one tear is dropped, one moment of despair allowed, and then "on with the story." She has a spirit that loves to breast the storm. She delights in the exercise of her own powers. When she discovers that the man she has married in Virginia is her own brother she is violently disgusted; she insists upon leaving him; but as soon as she sets foot in Bristol, "I took the diversion of going to Bath, for as I was still far from being old so my humour, which was always gay, continued so to an extreme." Heartless she is not, nor can any one charge her with levity; but life delights her, and a heroine who lives has us all in tow. Moreover, her ambition has that slight strain of imagination in it which puts it in the category of the noble passions. Shrewd and practical of necessity, she is yet haunted by a desire for romance and for the quality which to her perception makes a man a gentleman. "It was really a true gallant spirit he was of, and it was the more grievous to me. 'Tis something of relief even to be undone by a man of honour rather than by a scoundrel," she writes when she had misled a highwayman as to the extent of her fortune. It is in keeping with this temper that she should be proud of her final partner because he refuses to work when they reach the plantations but prefers hunting, and that she should take pleasure in buying him wigs and silver-hilted swords "to make him appear, as he really was, a very fine gentleman." Her very love of hot weather is in keeping, and the passion with which she kissed the ground that her son had trod on, and her noble tolerance of every kind of fault so long as it is not "complete baseness of spirit, imperious, cruel, and relentless when uppermost, abject and low-spirited when down." For the rest of the world she has nothing but good-will.

Since the list of the qualities and graces of this seasoned old sinner is by no means exhausted we can well understand how it was that Borrow's apple-woman on London Bridge called her "blessed Mary" and valued her book above all the apples on her stall; and that Borrow, taking the book deep into the booth, read till his eyes ached. But we dwell upon such signs of character only by way of proof that the creator of Moll Flanders was not, as he has been accused of being, a mere journalist and literal recorder of facts with no conception of the nature of psychology. It is true that his characters take shape and substance of their own accord, as if in despite of the author and not altogether to his liking. He never lingers or stresses any point of subtlety or pathos, but presses on imperturbably as if they came there without his knowledge. A touch of imagination, such as that when the Prince sits by his son's cradle and Roxana observes how "he loved to look at it when it was asleep," seems to mean much more to us than to him. After the curiously modern dissertation upon the need of communicating matters of importance to a second person lest, like the thief in Newgate, we should talk of it in our sleep, he apologises for his digression. He seems to have taken his characters so deeply into his mind that he lived them without exactly knowing how; and, like all unconscious artists, he leaves more gold in his work than his own generation was able to bring to the surface.

The interpretation that we put on his characters might therefore well have puzzled him. We find for ourselves meanings which he was careful to disguise even from his own eye. Thus it comes about that we admire Moll Flanders far more than we blame her. Nor can we believe that Defoe had made up his mind as to the precise degree of her guilt, or was unaware that in considering the lives of the abandoned he raised many deep questions and hinted, if he did not state, answers quite at variance with his professions of belief. From the evidence supplied by his essay upon the "Education of Women" we know that he had thought deeply and much in advance of his age upon the capacities of women, which he rated very high, and the injustice done to them, which he rated very harsh.

> I have often thought of it as one of the most barbarous customs in the world, considering us as a civilised and a Christian country, that we deny the advantages of learning to women. We reproach the sex every day with folly and impertinence; which I am confident, had they the advantages of education equal to us, they would be guilty of less than ourselves.

The advocates of women's rights would hardly care, perhaps, to claim Moll Flanders and Roxana among their patron saints; and yet it is clear that Defoe not only intended them to speak some very modern doctrines upon the subject, but placed them in circumstances where their peculiar hardships are displayed in such a way as to elicit our sympathy. Courage, said Moll Flanders, was what women needed, and the power to "stand their ground"; and at once gave practical demonstration of the benefits that would result. Roxana, a lady of the same profession, argues more subtly against the slavery of marriage. She "had started a new thing in the world" the merchant told her; "it was a way of arguing contrary to the general practise." But Defoe is the last writer to be guilty of bald preaching. Roxana keeps our attention because she is blessedly unconscious that she is in any good sense an example to her sex and is thus at liberty to own that part of her argument is "of an elevated strain which was really not in my thoughts at first, at all." The knowledge of her own frailties and the honest questioning of her own motives, which that knowledge begets, have the happy result of keeping her fresh and human when the martyrs and pioneers of so many problem novels have shrunken and shrivelled to the pegs and props of their respective creeds.

But the claim of Defoe upon our admiration does not rest upon the fact that he can be shown to have anticipated some of the views of Meredith, or to have written scenes which (the odd suggestion occurs) might have been turned into plays by Ibsen. Whatever his ideas upon the position of women, they are an incidental result of his chief virtue, which is that he deals with the important and lasting side of things and not with the passing and trivial. He is often dull.

He can imitate the matter-of-fact precision of a scientific traveller until
we wonder that his pen could trace or his brain conceive what has not
even the excuse of truth to soften its dryness. He leaves out the whole
of vegetable nature, and a large part of human nature. All this we may
admit, though we have to admit defects as grave in many writers whom
we call great. But that does not impair the peculiar merit of what
remains. Having at the outset limited his scope and confined his ambitions he achieves a truth of insight which is far rarer and more enduring than the truth of fact which he professed to make his aim. Moll
Flanders and her friends recommended themselves to him not because
they were, as we should say, "picturesque"; nor, as he affirmed, because they were examples of evil living by which the public might
profit. It was their natural veracity, bred in them by a life of hardship,
that excited his interest. For them there were no excuses; no kindly
shelter obscured their motives. Poverty was their taskmaster. Defoe
did not pronounce more than a judgement of the lips upon their fail-
ings. But their courage and resource and tenacity delighted him. He
found their society full of good talk, and pleasant stories, and faith
in each other, and morality of a home-made kind. Their fortunes had
that infinite variety which he praised and relished and beheld with
wonder in his own life. These men and women, above all, were free
to talk openly of the passions and desires which have moved men
and women since the beginning of time, and thus even now they keep
their vitality undiminished. There is a dignity in everything that is
looked at openly. Even the sordid subject of money, which plays so
large a part in their histories, becomes not sordid but tragic when it
stands not for ease and consequence but for honour, honesty, and life
itself. You may object that Defoe is humdrum, but never that he is
engrossed with petty things.

He belongs, indeed, to the school of the great plain writers, whose
work is founded upon a knowledge of what is most persistent, though
not most seductive, in human nature. The view of London from Hun-
gerford Bridge, grey, serious, massive, and full of the subdued stir of
traffic and business, prosaic if it were not for the masts of the ships
and the towers and domes of the city, brings him to mind. The tattered
girls with violets in their hands at the street corners, and the old
weather-beaten women patiently displaying their matches and boot-
laces beneath the shelter of arches, seem like characters from his books.
He is of the school of Crabbe and of Gissing, and not merely a fellow-
pupil in the same stern place of learning, but its founder and master.

Defoe As Novelist: *Moll Flanders*

by Ian Watt

Here is an episode from the later life of Moll Flanders as a thief:

> The next thing of moment was an attempt at a gentlewoman's gold watch. It happened in a crowd, at a meeting house, where I was in very great danger of being taken. I had full hold of her watch, but giving a great jostle as if somebody had thrust me against her, and in the juncture giving the watch a fair pull, I found it would not come, so I let it go that moment, and cried as if I had been killed, that somebody had trod upon my foot, and that there was certainly pickpockets there, for somebody or other had given a pull at my watch; for you are to observe that on these adventures we always went very well dressed, and I had very good clothes on, and a gold watch by my side, as like a lady as other folks.
>
> I had no sooner said so but the other gentlewoman cried out, "A Pickpocket," too, for somebody, she said, had tried to pull her watch away.
>
> When I touched her watch I was close to her, but when I cried out I stopped as it were short, and the crowd bearing her forward a little, she made a noise too, but it was at some distance from me, so that she did not in the least suspect me; but when she cried out, "A Pickpocket," somebody cried out, "Ay, and here has been another; this gentlewoman has been attempted too."
>
> At that very instant, a little farther in the crowd, and very luckily too, they cried out, "A Pickpocket," again, and really seized a young fellow in the very fact. This, though unhappy for the wretch, was very opportunely for my case, though I had carried it handsomely enough before; but now it was out of doubt, and all the loose part of the crowd ran that way, and the poor boy was delivered up to the rage of the street, which is a cruelty I need not describe, and which however, they are always glad of, rather than be sent to Newgate, where they lie often a long time and sometimes they are hanged, and the best they can look for, if they are convicted is to be transported.

It is very convincing. The gold watch is a real object, and it won't come, even with "a fair pull." The crowd is composed of solid bodies,

From "Defoe As Novelist: Moll Flanders." From The Rise of the Novel *by Ian Watt (Berkeley and Los Angeles: University of California Press; London: Hogarth Press, Ltd., 1957), pp. 96–101, 108–10, 113–15, 121–26, 130–31. Reprinted by permission of The Regents of the University of California and Chatto & Windus, Ltd.*

pushing forwards and backwards, and lynching another pickpocket in the street outside. All this happens in a real, particular place. It is true that, as is his custom, Defoe makes no attempt to describe it in detail, but the little glimpses that emerge win us over completely to its reality. A dissenting meeting-house is a piquant choice for these activities, to be sure, but Defoe does not arouse suspicion that he is a literary man by drawing attention to its ironic inappropriateness.

If we have any doubts, they are concerned, not with the authenticity of the episode, but with its literary status. The vividness of the scene itself is curiously incidental. Defoe gets into the middle of the action, with "I had full hold of her watch," and then suddenly changes from laconic reminiscent summary to a more detailed and immediate presentation, as though only to back up the truth of his initial statement. Nor has the scene been planned as a coherent whole: we are soon interrupted in the middle of the scene by an aside explaining something that might have been explained before, the important fact that Moll Flanders was dressed like a gentlewoman herself: this transition adds to our trust that no ghost-writer has been imposing order on Moll Flanders's somewhat rambling reminiscences, but if we had seen Moll dressed "as like a lady as other folks" from the beginning, the action would have run more strongly, because uninterruptedly, into the next incident of the scene—the raising of the alarm.

Defoe goes on to stress the practical moral, which is that the gentlewoman should have "seized the next body that was behind her," instead of crying out. In so doing, Defoe lives up to the didactic purpose professed in the "Author's Preface," but at the same time he directs our attention to the important problem of what the point of view of the narrator is supposed to be. We presume that it is a repentant Moll, speaking towards the end of her life: it is therefore surprising that in the next paragraph she should gaily describe her "governess's" procuring activities as "pranks." Then a further confusion about the point of view becomes apparent: we notice that to Moll Flanders other pickpockets, and the criminal fraternity in general, are a "they," not a "we." She speaks as though she were not implicated in the common lot of criminals; or is it, perhaps, Defoe who has unconsciously dropped into the "they" he himself would naturally use for them? And earlier, when we are told that "the other gentlewoman" cried out, we wonder why the word "other"? Is Moll Flanders being ironical about the fact that she too was dressed like a gentlewoman, or has Defoe forgotten that, actually, she is not?

Nor are these doubts about the completeness of Defoe's control over his narrative dispelled by the relationship, or rather lack of relationship, between this passage and the rest of the book. The transition to the next episode is somewhat confusing. It is effected, first by the address to the reader explaining how to deal with pickpockets, and then by a somewhat confusing *résumé* of the governess's life which is introduced by the words: "I had another adventure, which puts this matter out of doubt, and which may be an instruction for posterity in the case of a pickpocket." We and posterity, however, remain uninstructed, since the ensuing adventure turns out to be concerned with shoplifting: it seems likely that Defoe did not have the end of his paragraph in mind when he began it, and improvised an expository transition to mark time until some other incident suggested itself.

The connection between the meeting-house scene and the narrative as a whole confirms the impression that Defoe paid little attention to the internal consistency of his story. When she is transported to Virginia Moll Flanders gives her son a gold watch as a memento of their reunion; she relates how she "desired he would now and then kiss it for my sake," and then adds sardonically that she did not tell him "that I stole it from a gentlewoman's side, at a meeting house in London." Since there is no other episode in *Moll Flanders* dealing with watches, gentlewomen and meeting-houses, we must surely infer that Defoe had a faint recollection of what he had written a hundred pages earlier about the attempt on the gentlewoman's gold watch, but forgot that it had failed.

These discontinuities strongly suggest that Defoe did not plan his novel as a coherent whole, but worked piecemeal, very rapidly, and without any subsequent revision. This is indeed very likely on other grounds. His main aim as a writer was certainly to achieve a large and effective output—over fifteen hundred pages of print in the year that saw *Moll Flanders*; and this output was not primarily intended for a careful and critical audience. That Defoe had very little of the author's usual fastidious attitude to his work, or even of the author's sensitiveness to adverse criticism, is very evident from the terms of his prefatory apology for the poetic imperfections of the work of which he was perhaps most proud, *The True-Born Englishman*: ". . . without being taken for a conjuror, I may venture to foretell, that I shall be cavilled at about my mean style, rough verse, and incorrect language, things I indeed might have taken more care in. But the book is printed; and though I see some faults, it is too late to mend them. And this is all I think needful to say . . ." If Defoe was as nonchalant as this about an early work, and a poem at that, it is surely unlikely that he gave a second thought to the possible inconsistencies in a work of popular fiction such as *Moll Flanders*; especially as, for such an ill-regarded and ephemeral kind of writing, his publisher would probably not have offered the extra payment which Defoe would apparently have required for revising his manuscript.

Defoe's very casual attitude to his writing goes far to explain the inconsistencies in matters of detail which are very common in all his works; the same lack of coherent initial plan or of later revision can be surmised in the nature of his narrative method.

Nearly all novels employ a combination of two different methods of reporting: relatively full scenic presentation where, at a definite time and place, the doings of the characters are reported more or less fully; and passages of barer and less detailed summary which set the stage and provide a necessary connective framework. The tendency of most novelists is to reduce these latter synopses to a minimum and to focus as much attention as possible on a few fully realised scenes; but this is not the case with Defoe. His story is told in over a hundred realised scenes whose average length is less than two pages, and an equally large number of passages containing rapid and often perfunctory connective synopses.

The effect is obvious: almost every page offers evidence of the fall in tension as we switch from episode to summary—for a minute Moll Flanders will appear brilliantly illumined, only to fall back into the semi-darkness of confused recollection. It is certain that it is the fully presented episodes which include all that is vivid and memorable in *Moll Flanders,* and which are rightly quoted by enthusiasts as evidence of Defoe's narrative genius; but they surely forget how large a proportion of the book is occupied by uninspired summary, plaster over an inordinate number of cracks. Defoe, certainly, makes no effort to reduce the amount of patchwork required by consolidating the episodes into as large units as possible. The first main group of episodes, for example, when Moll is seduced by the Elder Brother, is divided into a very large number of separate encounters between the characters concerned, each of whose effectiveness is largely dissipated as the narrative relapses into bare summary. Similarly Moll's reaction to the discovery of the incestuous nature of her marriage to her half-brother is split up into so many separate scenes that the emotional force of the episode as a whole is much weakened.

This somewhat primitive aspect of Defoe's narrative technique is partly a reflection of the nature of his basic literary purpose—to produce a convincing likeness to the autobiographical memoir of a real person; and it will therefore require further examination in this larger context. First, however, the present analysis of the meeting-house passage must be concluded by a brief consideration of what is surely its most strikingly successful aspect—its prose.

Defoe's prose is not in the ordinary sense well-written, but it is remarkably effective in keeping us very close to the consciousness of Moll Flanders as she struggles to make her recollection clear: as we read we feel that nothing but an exclusive concentration on this single aim could account for such complete disregard of normal stylistic considerations—the repetitions and parentheses, the unpremeditated and sometimes stumbling rhythm, the long and involved sequences of co-ordinate clauses. The length of the sentences might at first sight seem to interfere with the effect of spontaneous authenticity; but in fact the lack of marked pauses within the sentences, and the frequent recapitulations, tend to heighten the effect.

The most remarkable thing about the prose of the passage is perhaps the fact that it is Defoe's usual style. No previous author's normal way of writing could so credibly have passed for the characteristic utterance of such an uneducated person as Moll Flanders. . . .

Moll Flanders is certainly, as E. M. Forster says, a novel of character;[1] the plot throws the whole burden of interest on the heroine, and many readers have felt that she supports it triumphantly. On the other hand, Leslie Stephen has reproached Defoe with a lack of "all that goes by the name of psychological analysis in modern fiction," [2] and not altogether without justification, at least if our emphasis is on the word analysis. There is probably no episode in *Moll Flanders* where the motivation is unconvincing, but for somewhat damaging reasons—few of the situations confronting Defoe's heroine call for any more complex discriminations than those of Pavlov's dog: Defoe makes us admire the speed and resolution of Moll's reactions to profit or danger; and if there are no detailed psychological analyses, it is because they would be wholly superfluous.

There are two main ways in which later novelists have manifested their powers of psychological understanding: indirectly, by revealing the character's personality through his actions; or directly, by specific analysis of the character's various states of mind. Both these methods, of course, can be and usually are combined; and they are usually found in conjunction with a narrative structure designed to embody the character's development, and to present him with crucial moral choices which bring his whole personality into play. There is very little of these things in *Moll Flanders*. Defoe does not so much portray his heroine's character as assume its reality in every action, and carry his reader with him—if we accede to the reality of the deed, it is difficult to challenge the reality of the doer. It is only when we attempt to fit all her acts together, and see them as an expression of a single personality, that doubts arise; nor are these doubts allayed when we discover how little we are told about some of the things we should need to know for a full picture of her personality, and how some of the things we are told seem contradictory.

These deficiencies are especially apparent in Defoe's treatment of

[1] *Aspects of the Novel* [(New York: Harcourt, Brace, Inc., 1954; first published 1927)], p. 61.
[2] "Defoe's Novels," [in *Hours in a Library* (New York, 1892)], p. 17.

personal relationships. We are told very little, for example, about the quality of Moll Flanders's loves, and even our information about their quantity is suspiciously meagre. When she accuses herself of having "lain with thirteen men," we cannot but resent the fact that some six lovers have been hidden not only from her fifth husband, but, much more unforgiveably, from us. Even among those lovers we know, we cannot be sure which Moll preferred. We have a strong impression that James is her favourite, and that she leaves him for the fifth or banking one only out of dire economic necessity; yet she tells us that on her honeymoon with the latter she "never lived four pleasanter days together," and that five years of an "uninterrupted course of ease and content" ensued. When James later reappears, however, our earlier impression recurs with renewed force:

> He turned pale, and stood speechless, like one thunderstruck, and, not able to conquer the surprise, said no more but this, "Let me sit down"; and sitting down by a table, he laid his elbow on the table, and leaning his head on his hand, fixed his eyes on the ground as one stupid. I cried so vehemently, on the other hand, that it was a good while ere I could speak any more; but after I had given some vent to my passion by tears, I repeated the same words, "My dear, do you not know me?" At which he answered, Yes, and said no more a good while.

Defoe's laconic narrative manner could be supremely evocative when it was focussed on personal relationships, but this happened rather rarely, probably because neither Defoe nor Moll Flanders conceived of such intangible concerns as important and continuing elements in human life. We are certainly given very little help in understanding Moll's conflicting feelings during her marriage with the banker. Like the first two husbands, he is individualised only to the extent of being given an ordinal number; and Moll's life with him is treated as a brief and wholly self-contained episode whose emotional premise does not have to be reconciled with other features of her life and character. Defoe, indeed, emphasises this discontinuity by telling us that James wrote three times to Moll at this time suggesting that they go off to Virginia as she had earlier proposed, but only after the fifth husband has been long dead: another novelist would have made such pleas an opportunity for clarifying his heroine's conflicting feelings towards the two men, but Defoe gives us only the bare facts, long after they have lost their potential power for psychological illumination.

If we attempt to draw any conclusion from Defoe's treatment of these particular personal relationships it must surely be that Moll Flanders was unaffectedly happy with both husbands, and that although her love of one of them was deeper, she did not allow this sentiment to interfere with the solid comforts which the other was able to provide. She is, obviously, affectionate but no sentimentalist. We get a somewhat different picture, however, when we come to consider her character, not as a wife, but as a mother. On the one hand, she can behave with complete sentimental abandon, as when she kisses the ground her long-separated son Humphry has been standing on; on the other hand, although she shows some fondness for two or three of her children, she is by normal standards somewhat callous in her treatment of most of them—the majority are mentioned only to be forgotten, and, once left in the care of relatives or foster mothers, are neither redeemed subsequently nor even inquired after when opportunity permits. Here the conclusion about her character must surely be that, although there are extenuating circumstances, she is often a heartless mother. It is difficult to see how this can be reconciled either with her kissing the ground that Humphry has trodden, or with the fact that she herself loudly condemns unnatural mothers, but never makes any such accusation against herself even in her deepest moments of penitent self-reprobation. . . .

If none of those close to Moll Flanders seem at all aware of her true character, and if we continue to suspect that her own account of herself may be partial, our only remaining resource for an objective view of her personality is Defoe himself. Here again, however, we at once encounter difficulties. For Moll Flanders is suspiciously like her author, even in matters where we would expect striking and obvious differences. The facts show that she is a woman and a criminal, for example; but neither of these roles determines her personality as Defoe has drawn it.

Moll Flanders, of course, has many feminine traits; she has a keen eye for fine clothes and clean linen, and shows a wifely concern for the creature comforts of her males. Further, the early pages of the book undoubtedly present a young girl with a lifelike clarity, and later there are many touches of a rough cockney humour that is undeniably feminine in tone. But these are relatively external and minor matters, and the essence of her character and actions is, to one reader at least, essentially masculine. This is a personal impression, and would be difficult, if not impossible, to establish: but it is at least certain that Moll accepts none of the disabilities of her sex, and indeed one cannot but feel that Virginia Woolf's admiration for her was largely due to admiration of a heroine who so fully realised one of the ideals of feminism: freedom from any involuntary involvement in the feminine role.

Moll Flanders is also similar to her author in another respect: she seems fundamentally untouched by her criminal background, and, on the contrary, displays many of the attitudes of a virtuous and public-minded citizen. Here, again, there is no glaring inconsistency, but there is a marked pattern of attitudes which distinguishes Moll from other members of her class: in the passage quoted above she showed no

fellow-feeling for the boy pickpocket; later she is full of virtuous indignation at the "hardened wretches" of Newgate, and they repay in kind
by hooting at her derisively; and when finally she is transported she
has the satisfaction of observing, from her privileged comfort in the
captain's quarters, that the "old fraternity" are "kept under hatches."
Moll Flanders obviously places criminals into two classes: most of
them are vicious reprobates who richly deserve their fate; but she and
a few of her friends are essentially virtuous and deserving people who
have been unfortunate—she is even morally pure in her whoring since
it is, as she assures us, by necessity and not "for the sake of the vice."
Like Defoe, in fact, she is a good Puritan who, despite a few necessary
and regrettable compromises, has, in the main and in defiance of illus-
trious precedent, lived in a world of pitch and not been defiled.

It is this freedom from the probable psychological and social consequences of everything she does which is the central implausibility of
her character as Defoe has drawn it. It applies, not only to her crimes,
but to everything she does. If we take the incest theme, for example, we
find that although her half brother becomes incapable in body and
mind mainly because Moll Flanders has left him, after revealing her
terrible secret, she herself is quite unaffected by the circumstance, once
she has left Virginia. Nor are her son's feelings towards her influenced,
apparently, by the fact that he is the offspring of an incestuous marriage; nor even by the fact that his mother, after deserting him for
some twenty years, only returns because, having been transported back
to his vicinity, she thinks that she may now have an estate to inherit,
an estate which he would otherwise enjoy.

Moll Flanders's character, then, is not noticeably affected either by
her sex, by her criminal pursuits, or indeed by any of the objective
factors which might have been expected to set her apart from her
author; on the other hand, she shares with Defoe and most of his
heroes many of the character traits that are usually regarded as middle-
class. She is obsessed with gentility and keeping up appearances; her
pride is much involved in knowing how to get good service and proper
accommodation; and she is in her heart a rentier, for whom life has no
greater terror than when her "main stock wastes apace." More specifically it is apparent that, like Robinson Crusoe, she has, by some
process of osmosis, picked up the vocabulary and attitudes of a tradesman. Indeed her most positive qualities are the same as Crusoe's, a
restless, amoral and strenuous individualism. It is, no doubt, possible
to argue that these qualities might be found in a character of her sex,
station and personal vicissitudes; but it is not likely, and it is surely
more reasonable to assume that all these contradictions are the consequence of a process to which first-person narration is peculiarly prone;
that Defoe's identification with Moll Flanders was so complete that,

despite a few feminine traits, he created a personality that was in essence his own. . . .

Moll Flanders has a few examples of patent and conscious irony. There is, first of all, a good deal of dramatic irony of a simple kind: for example in Virginia, where a woman relates the story of Moll's incestuous marriage, not knowing that she is addressing its chief figure. There are also some examples of much more pointed irony, as in the passage when, as a little girl, Moll Flanders vows that she will become a gentlewoman when she grows up, like one of her leisured but scandalous neighbours:

> "Poor child," says my good old nurse, "you may soon be such a gentlewoman as that, for she is a person of ill fame, and has had two bastards."
> I did not understand anything of that; but I answered, "I am sure they call her madam, and she does not go to service nor do housework"; and therefore I insisted that she was a gentlewoman, and I would be such a gentlewoman as that.

It is good dramatic irony to point this prophetic episode with the phrase "such a gentlewoman as that," where the verbal emphasis also drives home the difference between virtue and class, and the moral dangers of being taken in by external evidences of gentility. We can be certain that the irony is conscious because its tenor is supported by Defoe's other writings, which often show a somewhat rancorous spirit towards the failure of the gentry to provide proper models of conduct: there is a similar tendency, for example, in Moll's later ironical description of the eldest brother as "a gay gentleman who . . . had levity enough to do an ill-natured thing, yet had too much judgment of things to pay too dear for his pleasures." Here, the combination of stylistic elegance and demonstrable consonance with Defoe's own point of view makes us sure that Moll Flanders's reflection after she has been duped by James is also ironical: " 'Tis something of relief even to be undone by a man of honour, rather than by a scoundrel." The verbal hyperbole drives home the contrast between overt and actual moral norms: "undone" is a calculated exaggeration, Moll Flanders being what she is already; and the ambiguity of "a man of honour" seems to be used with full consciousness of its subversive effect.

These examples of conscious irony in *Moll Flanders*, however, fall far short of the larger, structural irony which would suggest that Defoe viewed either his central character or his purported moral theme ironically. There is certainly nothing in *Moll Flanders* which clearly indicates that Defoe sees the story differently from the heroine. . . .

The lack of insulation between incongruous attitudes seems particularly ironical if we are already predisposed to regard one of them as false. This happens with many of the moralising passages, and Defoe

certainly does nothing to obviate our incredulity by the way he introduces them. One glaringly improbable case occurs when an as yet
impenitent Moll relates to the governess how she was picked up by a
drunken man whom she later robbed, and goes on to improve the
occasion by quoting Solomon in the course of a lay sermon against
drunkenness. The governess is much moved, Moll tells us:

> . . . it so affected her that she was hardly able to forbear tears, to think
> how such a gentleman ran a daily risk of being undone, every time a
> glass of wine got into his head.
>
> But as to the purchase I got, and how entirely I stripped him, she told
> me it pleased her wonderfully. "Nay, child," says she, "the usage may,
> for aught I know, do more to reform him than all the sermons that ever
> he will hear in his life." And if the remainder of the story be true, so it
> did.

The two women then combine to anticipate divine retribution, and
to milk the poor gentleman of his cash, in order to drive their lesson
home. The episode is certainly a travesty of piety and morality; and
yet it is very unlikely that Defoe is being ironical; any more than he
is later when, by some very human obliquity, Moll Flanders excuses
herself from the prison chaplain's appeal that she confess her sins on
the grounds of his addiction to the bottle. Both episodes are plausible
enough psychologically: the devotees of one vice are often less char-
itable than the virtuous about the other ones they happen not to
favour. The problem, however, is whether Defoe himself overlooked,
and expected his readers to overlook, the very damaging nature of the
context in which his homilies against alcohol occur. There is every
reason to believe that he did: the lesson itself must have been intended
seriously, and not ironically; as for its context, we have already seen
that there was no way in which Defoe could make good his didactic
professions except by making Moll double as chorus for his own honest
beliefs; and there is therefore good reason to believe that the moral
imperceptiveness which is so laughably clear to us is in fact a reflection
of one of the psychological characteristics of Puritanism which Defoe
shared with his heroine.

Svend Ranulf, in his *Moral Indignation and Middle Class Psychology*, has shown, mainly from Commonwealth pamphlets, how the
Puritans were much more addicted to outbursts of moral indignation
than were the Royalists.[3] One of the strengths of Puritanism, he suggests, lay in its tendency to convert its demand for righteousness into
a somewhat uncharitable aggressiveness against the sins of others: and
this, of course, carried with it a complementary tendency for the individual to be mercifully blind to his own faults. Moll Flanders fre-

[3] Copenhagen, 1938, especially pp. 94, 198.

quently exemplifies this tendency. One famous instance is the passage
when she consoles herself for having stolen a child's gold necklace
with the reflection: "I only thought I had given the parents a just
reproof for their negligence, in leaving the poor lamb to come home
by itself, and it would teach them to take more care another time."
There is no doubt about the psychological veracity of the reflection:
the conscience is a great casuist. There is, however, some doubt about
Defoe's intention: is it meant to be an ironical touch about his
heroine's moral duplicities, her tendency to be blind to the beam in
her own eye? or did Defoe forget Moll as he raged inwardly at the
thought of how careless parents are, and how richly they deserve to be
punished?

If Defoe intended the passage to be an ironical portrayal of spiritual
self-deception, it becomes necessary to assume that he saw Moll
Flanders's character as a whole in this light, for the incident is typical
of her general blindness to her own spiritual and mental dishonesty.
She always lies about her financial position, for instance, even to those
she loves. Thus when the mutual trickery with James is revealed, she
conceals a thirty-pound bank-bill "and that made freer of the rest, in
consideration of his circumstances, for I really pitied him heartily."
Then she goes on, "But to return to this question, I told him I never
willingly deceived him and I never would." Later, after his departure,
she says: "Nothing that ever befell me in my life sank so deep into my
heart as this farewell. I reproached him a thousand times in my
thoughts for leaving me, for I would have gone with him through the
world, if I had begged my bread. I felt in my pocket, and there I found
ten guineas, his gold watch, and two little rings. . . ." She cannot even
in theory attest the reality of her devotion by expressing her willing-
ness to beg her bread, without immediately proving that it was only a
rhetorical hyperbole by reassuring herself that she has enough in her
pocket to keep her in bread for a lifetime. There is surely no conscious
irony here: for Defoe and his heroine generous sentiments are good,
and concealed cash reserves are good too, perhaps better; but there is
no feeling that they conflict, or that one attitude undermines the other.

Defoe had accused the occasional conformists of "playing Bo-Peep
with God Almighty."[4] The term admirably describes the politic equivo-
cations about common honesty and moral truth so common in *Moll
Flanders.* Defoe there "plays Bo-Peep" at various levels: from the
sentence and the incident to the fundamental ethical structure of the
whole book, his moral attitude to his creation is as shallow and devious
and easily deflected as his heroine's on the occasion when her married
gallant writes to her to terminate the affair, and urges her to change

⁴ *True Collection* . . . , p. 315.

her ways, she writes: "I was struck with this letter, as with a thousand wounds; the reproaches of my own conscience were such as I cannot express, for I was not blind to my own crime; and I reflected that I might with less offence have continued with my brother, since there was no crime in our marriage on that score, neither of us knowing it."

No writer who had allowed himself to contemplate either his heroine's conscience, or the actual moral implications of her career, in a spirit of irony, could have written this seriously. Nor could he have written the account of James's moral reformation, in which Moll Flanders tells us how she brought him the riches given by her son, not forgetting "the horses, hogs, and cows, and other stores for our plantation" and concludes "from this time forward I believe he was as sincere a penitent and as thoroughly a reformed man as ever God's goodness brought back from a profligate, a highwayman, and a robber." We, not Defoe, are ironically aware of the juxtaposition of the powers of God and Mammon; we, not Defoe, laugh at the concept of reformation through hogs and cows.

Whatever disagreement there may be about particular instances, it is surely certain that there is no consistently ironical attitude present in *Moll Flanders*. Irony in its extended sense expresses a deep awareness of the contradictions and incongruities that beset man in this vale of tears, an awareness which is manifested in the text's purposeful susceptibility to contradictory interpretations. As soon as we have become aware of the author's ulterior purpose, we can see all the apparent contradictions as indications of the coherent attitude underlying the whole work. Such a way of writing obviously makes severe demands upon the attention of the author and the reader: the implication of every word, the juxtaposition of every episode, the relation of every part to the whole, all must exclude any interpretation except the intended one. It is, as we have seen, very unlikely that Defoe wrote in this way, or that he had such readers; indeed, all the evidence points the other way. . . .

. . . Later novelists such as Jane Austen and Flaubert were to incorporate such conflicts and incongruities into the very structure of their works: they created irony, and made novel readers sensitive to its effects. We cannot but approach Defoe's novels through the literary expectations which later masters of the form made possible, and these expectations seem to find some justification as a result of our acute awareness of the conflicting nature of the two main forces in Defoe's philosophy of life—rational economic individualism and concern for spiritual redemption—which together held his divided but not, apparently, uneasy allegiance. Nevertheless, if we are primarily concerned with Defoe's actual intentions, we must conclude that although he reveals the sophistries whereby these dual allegiances are preserved intact, he does not, strictly speaking, portray them; consequently *Moll Flanders* is undoubtedly an ironic object, but it is not a work of irony.

The preceding sections are not intended as a denial of the importance of Defoe as a novelist, but only as a demonstration of a fact that might perhaps have been taken for granted if it had not been challenged or overlooked by many recent critics: the fact that Defoe's novels lack both the consistency in matters of detail of which many lesser writers are capable, and the larger coherences found in the greatest literature. Defoe's forte was the brilliant episode. Once his imagination seized on a situation he could report it with a comprehensive fidelity which was much in advance of any previous fiction, and which, indeed, has never been surpassed. These episodes are irresistible in quotation; and the pre-eminence of *Moll Flanders* is perhaps mainly due to its strong claim to be not so much a great novel as Defoe's richest anthology.

How far we should allow Defoe's gift for the perfect episode to outweigh his patent shortcomings—weaknesses of construction, inattention to detail, lack of moral or formal pattern—is a very difficult critical problem. There is something about Defoe's genius which is as confident and indestructible as the resilient selfhood of his heroine, and which all but persuades us to accept the notorious critical heresy that the single talent well employed can make up for all the others.

The talent, of course, is the supreme one in the novel: Defoe is the master illusionist, and this almost makes him the founder of the new form. Almost, but not quite: the novel could be considered established only when realistic narrative was organised into a plot which, while retaining Defoe's lifelikeness, also had an intrinsic coherence; when the novelist's eye was focussed on character and personal relationships as essential elements in the total structure, and not merely as subordinate instruments for furthering the verisimilitude of the actions described; and when all these were related to a controlling moral intention. It was Richardson who took these further steps, and it is primarily for this reason that he, rather than Defoe, is usually regarded as the founder of the English novel.

On *Moll Flanders*

by Dorothy Van Ghent

The editorial preface to a popular modern reprint of *Moll Flanders* speaks of the book as "one of the most remarkable examples of true realism in the whole range of fiction." The statement suggests that "true realism" is specifically that kind of realism which *Moll Flanders* exhibits; by implication, other kinds—if there are other kinds—would not be "true." There can be no gainsaying the realism of *Moll Flanders*: Defoe's book describes minutely the local scene, London; it refers circumstantially to contemporary customs (although not to those of the mid-seventeenth century in which Moll supposedly had her career, but to those of the early eighteenth century when Defoe was writing); it employs "documents" (Moll's "memorandums," quoted letters, hospital bills, etc.) in order to increase the illusion of verifiable fact; and, in general, it aims at "objective," "reportorial," "photographic" representation, as if from the standpoint of an artless observer. In other words, the whole book is oriented toward what we call "facts"—specifically toward those "facts" which are events and objects that have spatial-temporal determination. But it is unfortunate that factual orientation in the novel should have come to determine the definition of realism in the novel; for "realism" inevitably implies a doctrine of the "real"; and it implies, when it is used to describe the factually oriented novel, that spatial-temporal facts are the only "real," and therefore that the factually oriented novel is closer to "reality"—a more trustworthy representation of reality—than any other kind of novel. What is suggested by the statement quoted at the beginning of this essay is not an evaluation of *Moll Flanders* as literature, but a certain popular philosophical conviction of the exclusive "reality" of material facts, a conviction that the so-defined "realistic" novel seems to flatter and support; and what is blurred over by the statement is the *hypothetical* structure of even the most "documentary" or "circumstantial" kind of fiction, a hypothetical structure that it shares generically with all fiction.

"On Moll Flanders." *From* The English Novel: Form and Function *by Dorothy Van Ghent (New York: Holt, Rinehart and Winston, 1953), pp. 33–43. Copyright 1953 by Dorothy Van Ghent. Reprinted by permission of Holt, Rinehart and Winston, Inc.*

The hypothesis on which *Moll Flanders* is based might be phrased in this way: given a human creature "conditioned" to react only to material facts, then the world where that person lived might cogently assume the shape that Moll's world assumes—a shape astonishingly without spiritual dimension. In a parallel fashion one might phrase the hypothesis on which *The Pilgrim's Progress* is based: given a person for whom relationship with God was the only "reality," then, in his world, material facts would show as misleading appearances, and the shape taken by his adventures would be altogether spiritually dimensioned. If the world of the particular novel is to create itself fully for us, we must waive for the moment our own *a priori* convictions as to whether material fact or relationship with God is the prime reality; we must approach the fictional hypothesis with as much respect for its conditions and as much attention to its logic as we would give to a scientific or mathematical hypothesis. Defoe's "realism" must be looked upon as a consistent use of certain devices for the creation of a special kind of world, just as Bunyan's allegorical method is a consistent use of certain devices (some of them "realistic" in the same sense as Defoe's) for the creation of a special kind of world. Eventually, the trained and sensitized reader finds that novels called "realistic" are as symbolic as Bunyan's allegory.

The questions we must ask of *Moll Flanders* are those we ask of any other novel: what are its elements? how are they made to cohere in a unity? how are its special technical devices (in this case, those of "realism") appropriate to the making of this particular world? We notice, for instance, that Moll's world contains many *things*—tangible things such as watches and wigs and yardage goods and necklaces and dresses and barrels and bales and bottles and trunks. We may make some judgment as to the kind of world presented in a novel simply on the basis of the frequency with which an author uses certain substantives and images, to the exclusion of others. In *Moll,* there is relatively great frequency in the use of words naming that kind of object which constitutes material wealth. This singularity of *Moll Flanders* becomes striking when we try to remember how many dresses Christiana had for her long journey, and whether Mr. Worldly Wiseman wore a wig or carried a watch.

But let us make a further distinction: these tangible, material objects with which Moll is so deeply concerned are not at all vivid in texture. When Moll tells us that she put on a "good pearl necklace," we do not know whether the pearls were large or small or graded or uniform in size, or whether the necklace hung low on her bosom or was wound around her throat three times, nor do we know if the pearls were real or artificial; the word "good" here indicates simply that the pearls looked costly to a sophisticated eye, and were of a kind that a woman of substantial social position might wear; the "good pearl necklace" is mentioned not in a way that will make a sense image for us, but only in a way that will suggest the market value of the necklace and (through the market value) its value as an indicator of social prestige. Similarly, when she tells us that she gave her son a fine gold watch, we have no sense image of the watch; we do not know its size or design or delicacy or heft; we know only that it is a watch which would bring a good price. Therefore, in saying that the world of *Moll Flanders* is made up to a large extent of *things,* we do not mean that it is a world rich in physical, sensuous textures—in images for the eye or for the tactile sense or for the tongue or the ear or for the sense of temperature or the sense of pressure. It is extraordinarily barren of such images. And yet sense images are certainly "real" even in a world exclusively composed of "facts"; they are the constant means by which we are made aware of facts (the scientific observer himself is dependent upon their evidence). Clearly, then, an intense selectivity has limited the facts of Moll Flanders' world to a certain few kinds of facts, and has ignored great masses of other facts that we think of as making up the plenum of factual reality. Such selectivity warns us that this realistic novel is not actually an "objective," "reportorial," "photographic" representation of reality; its selectivity is that of the work of art, whose purpose is not that of an "objective" report.

What is important in Moll's world of things is the counting, measuring, pricing, weighing, and evaluating of the things in terms of the wealth they represent and the social status they imply for the possessor. What is unimportant (and we learn as much by what is unimportant as by what is important) is sensuous life, the concrete experience of things as they have individual texture. The unimportance of sensuous life in Moll's world is fairly astonishing inasmuch as Moll herself is a lusty, full-bodied, lively-sensed creature. Our instrument or medium of knowledge about Moll's world is Moll. The medium is a sensual medium (what woman, weak in sensuality, would remark, as Moll does: "I never was in bed with my husband, but I wished myself in the arms of his brother . . . in short, I committed adultery and incest with him every day in my desires . . ." or would have given us the scenes in the inns at Gloucester and Bath?); but communicated through this medium is an assemblage of objects entirely desensualized, inaccessible to sense, abstract—abstract because represented only by name and by market value on the commercial and social markets. We may speak of this contradiction as an irony, and we shall wish to use the word "irony" here as indicating one characteristic *mode of relationship between elements in a novelistic structure.* Irony can imply many kinds of discrepancy, contrast, contradiction; paradox is a form of irony; there is irony in a statement that appears to say one thing and actually signifies another; and there is irony in a life situation or in a story situation that contrasts with or contradicts what might be expected from certain of the circumstances. We are always aware of Moll's sensuality, even though it often lies subterraneously or at a subverbal level in the novel; a great many of her adventures are sexual; but the life of the flesh is faded completely by the glare of the life of the pocketbook; and the incipience of sensuality, its always latent presence, contrasts ironically with the meagerness and abstractness of a sensibility which frantically converts all sense experience into cash value.

We shall continue to speak of ironies in *Moll Flanders*, and as we shall be speaking of them as aspects of the book's internal structure, let us formulate what we mean by the structural function of irony. We shall do so most easily by analogy. A round arch is made up of a number of wedge-shaped blocks, and each of these blocks is pulled earthward in obedience to gravity, but each also exerts a sideways push against its neighbor because of its wedge shape and the weight of other blocks around and over it. If there were only the one pull, freely earthward, the blocks would fall and there would be no arch; but because of the counterforce, acting in the sideways direction, the structure of the arch is defined and preserved. The contrasting significances of an ironic statement or of an ironic situation may be compared with the counteracting stresses that hold the arch up and hold it together—that give it its structure. In *Moll Flanders,* a complex system of ironies or counterstresses holds the book together as a coherent and significant work of art. We may speak of the ironies, then, as "structural." In the example that we have cited, Moll's latent sensuality acts as a counterstress to her devotion to financial abstractions, and the cross-pulls of these two tendencies define Moll and her world meaningfully for us.

To illustrate further, let us follow some of her characteristic mental processes. Here is one chief inflection of her psychology—the reader will find it repeated again and again as he listens to her tale. It appears in her account of her first marriage, her marriage to the younger brother of her seducer. Five years she has been married to him, she has had two children by him, she has known a long and important period (important because she is still very young) of domesticity and marital tenderness and motherhood. How does she tell us of these matters?

> It concerns the story in hand very little to enter into the further particulars . . . only to observe that I had two children by him, and that at the end of the five years he died. He had been really a very good husband to me, and we lived very agreeably together; but as he had not received much from them [the parents], and had in the little time he lived acquired no great matters, so my circumstances were not great, nor was I much mended by the match. Indeed, I had preserved the elder brother's bonds to me to pay me £500, which he offered me for my con-

sent to marry his brother; and this, with what I had saved of the money
he formerly gave me, and about as much more by my husband, left me
a widow with about £1200 in my pocket.

We know in some degree from this context, and with added conviction
from other similar contexts, what Moll means by a "very good husband" and by saying that they lived "very agreeably": the man had
enough money to keep Moll from want, he spent money freely enough
to maintain her in comfort and in that kind of social respectability
which the spending of money guarantees—therefore he was "good"
and their life was "agreeable." Any other characterization of this husband or of their marital life we should not be able to guess at; for
Moll, simply by her exclusion of any other kind of perception from her
story, stringently limits our own imagination of character; and we must
judge that Moll has no other perception of character. The phrases
"received much," "acquired no great matters," "my circumstances were
not great," and "mended by the match," all focus together on one kind
of referent: money. And when we find similar phrases in other contexts, we shall expect that "much" and "matters" and "circumstances"
and "great" and "mended" (though these words might have immensely
different meanings in other books) will have the same common referent
again. As Moll uses them, they are very abstract words, colorless little
words, words as limited in meaning as a mathematical sign. By their
frequency they compose a picture of Moll's mentality and sensibility,
so exclusively focused, so narrow and intense, that if (conceivably) we
were offered the same description of symptoms in a clinical case history, we should say that it was a picture of a madwoman. But Moll's
is not a case history; it is a hypothesis of personality development in
an acquisitive world; and in this world Moll is by no means a clinical
subject—she is "well adjusted."

What five years of her young womanhood, marriage, domesticity, and
motherhood mean to Moll are certain finances, certain bonds amount-
ing to so much, a certain quantity of cash in her pocket. Of her children
by this husband, she says,

> My two children were, indeed, taken happily off my hands by my hus-
> band's father and mother, and that was all they got by Mrs. Betty.

The statement informs us, with powerful obliquity, that the way to be
happy through children is to have them taken off one's hands; it informs us also that children may be useful in settling family debts. With
the greatest placidity and aplomb on Moll's part, the children are
neatly converted into a shrewd price by which she gets out of a bad
bargain with clean skirts. Schematically, what has been happening here
is the conversion of all subjective, emotional, and moral experience—
implicit in the fact of Moll's five years of marriage and motherhood

—into pocket and bank money, into the materially measurable. It is a shocking formula, shocking in its simplicity and abruptness and entireness. It confronts us again with the irony, or system of ironies, that is structural to the book. A great mass of responses that might be expected from the circumstances (marriage, death, birth) is not what is presented; what is presented of that pyramid of human experience, as its only symbol and significance, is a cash sign. And yet another irony is involved: that is the paradox of Moll's superb "sanity," witnessed by her perfect "adjustment" to her world, and her violent abnormality as a representative of the species called human. A person is sane who is socially adapted in his time and his place, in tune with his culture, furnished with the mental and moral means to meet contingencies (to "mend" his circumstances, in Moll's phrase, when they need mending), accepting the values that his society accepts, and collaborating in their preservation. By these tokens, Moll is eminently sane. She is a collector of quantities of things and of cash, for in the world in which she lives, the having of things and of cash is necessary for survival; it is an expression of the will to live. She has one thing to sell, in order to obtain them, and that is her sex. When this commodity fails her, she simply takes the things and the cash—steals them. In either case, she shows her sanity, her "adjustment" to her world, her ability to meet all contingencies. In this sense she is "normal," exhibiting in her activities and attitudes the social norm of her world; in terms of the full emotional variety of what we think of as the "human," she is monstrously abnormal. Her abnormality is her exclusive abstractiveness as a counter of cash; her subjective life is sunken nearly to a zero.

What will Moll do when she is under severe emotional stress; that is, when there is nothing in her situation that she can abstract into numbers, measurements, cash value, and when whatever is left for her perception to work on is the internal or subjective life of feeling and emotion? At the crisis of her career, she is taken for thieving, put into Newgate prison; and Newgate is hell. We have only Moll's own words for this experience, and how are Moll's words—dictated by a perceptive apparatus adapted exclusively for enumerating and calculating— to describe hell for us? Hell, Milton's Satan said, is a place within the self; that is, it is a subjective place, a place defined by horror and suffering and deep distress of spirit. In all her other circumstances, Moll has never failed to describe and define with the utmost precision such experience as she is capable of. But the hell of Newgate is "impossible to describe." The impossible description of this dead end of human suffering she fills up with negatives, words denying any possibility of description, for she has only negatives and blank counters for the subjective.

. . . indeed, nothing could be filled with more horror . . . nothing was

more odious to me than the company that was there . . . indeed no
colours can represent that place to the life.

To get over these impossibilities, the hell of Newgate is expressed by
generalized reference to noises and smells (Newgate is most painful
because it is not "respectable"; there are loud noises and bad smells
here as there are in the slums), and by abstract stereotypes of fiendish-
ness.

> . . . the hellish noise, the roaring, swearing, and clamour, the stench
> and nastiness, and all the dreadful afflicting things that I saw there . . . ;
> I thought of nothing night or day, but of gibbets and halters, evil spirits
> and devils; it is not to be expressed how I was harassed . . .

With the intervention of the minister, Moll says she is "perfectly
changed," she becomes "another body." But since her perceptions are
limited to their familiar categories of number and quantity, suitable
for inventorying gold watches and bonds and purse change, but
scarcely suitable for the description of grief or guilt or purity, the
heaven of her repentance is as ineffable as the hell of Newgate. "The
word eternity," she says,

> represented itself with all its incomprehensible additions, and I had such
> extended notions of it that I know not how to express them. Among the
> rest, how absurd did every pleasant thing look!—I mean, that we had
> counted before—when I reflected that these sordid trifles were the things
> for which we forfeited eternal felicity.

But immediately, after these weightless matters, these incomprehensible
additions and extended notions, Moll and her husband are back at the
reckoning, the formulary conversion of death and birth, heaven and
hell, into cash.

> Our first business was to compare our stock. He was very honest to me,
> and told me his stock was pretty good . . . I gave him an account of
> my stock as faithfully . . . My stock which I had with me was £246
> some odd shillings; so that we had £354 between us . . .

With her heart lifted up in gratitude to Providence, Moll plans an irreproachable life, for an irreproachable life is now truly possible:
Christian virtue and "stock" have become metaphysically identified, an
eternal equation in the mysterious plan of things. From now on, God
punches the buttons of this cash-register world, and it is virtue that lies
in the till. Most grotesque of ironies: the "sordid trifles," the "pleasant
things" that now look so "absurd" to Moll, the things for which she
now refuses to forfeit her "eternal felicity," come to her henceforth in
greater quantities than ever before, precisely as the sign of grace and
redemption, the temporal guarantee of her eternal felicity.

In speaking of the structure of *Moll Flanders* in terms of a hierarchy of ironies—a system of stresses and counterstresses (to return to our figure of the arch) that "hold the book together" in significant unity—we are faced with the need, sooner or later, of making some tentative distinction between what the author might have intended ironically and what actually functions ironically in the book. This question, of the author's deliberate intention, arises particularly in connection with irony; for we think of an author as knowing what he is doing better than another person might know what he is doing, and if he is being elaborately ironic, then—one would assume—he must "intend" at least some of the irony. Irony is "double-talk." But if the author is "sincere" and intends no double-talk, would it not be more consistent usage, on our part, to say that the book is "sincere" in the same sense that the author is sincere, that it contains no double-talk, no ironies?

Let us illustrate this difficulty as it suggests itself in the specifically moralizing portions of *Moll Flanders*. Moll robs a child, comes near to murdering the infant, and moralizes the adventure thus:

> . . . as I did the poor child no harm, I only thought I had given the parents a just reproof for their negligence, in leaving the poor lamb to come home by itself, and it would teach them to take more care another time . . .

She rolls a drunk, after a night spent whoring, comes home to count and weigh her loot, and accompanies her highly satisfactory calculations with moving reflections on the sins which fathers visit upon their children by drunkenness and wenching; she is even inspired to quote Solomon on the foul disease. These reflections are followed by a complacent account of how the adventure, into which she had led the gentleman, had brought him to reform his ways, restored him to the bosom of a loving wife, and secured the happiness of an innocent family. It is to these moralizing thoughts of Moll's that Defoe is undoubtedly referring the reader, in his Author's Preface, when he advises us to make "virtuous and religious uses" of the story. He even mentions, in his Preface, the incident of the robbery of the little girl, and the moral message he associates with this incident is precisely that given it by Moll herself—parents who deck their children in finery and allow them to go to dancing school alone are given a "good memento" of what may ensue; and, generally, the moral that he would have us find in Moll's accounts of her criminal practices is that which Moll (now a reformed soul and "honest" woman at the time of writing her memoirs) is herself always anxious to inculcate. But what, objectively, is the relationship of Moll's moralizing thoughts to her adventures? Her adventures are criminal, but she herself is not a criminal type; she is not a woman of the underworld, but a woman of the bourgeois world; her aspirations are thoroughly middle-class—she wants, above all, economic security and middle-class respectability. She thinks middle-class thoughts; her morality is middle-class morality—platitudinous, stereotypic, a morality suited to the human species in its peculiar aspect as cash calculator, and a morality, therefore, most particularly suitable to the prostitute.

Criminal in action, Moll will have to moralize crime as a social good: and so she does. Her robbery of a child will have prevented many future crimes of this kind; her depredations upon one drunk will have preserved the happiness of many families: all the readers of *Moll Flanders* will have received her benefactions. Moll's moralizing thoughts are the harmonies of the cash-register world in which she lives, for the cash register, like the celestial spheres, has its harmonies too, as the buttons are punched, the mechanism throbs, and the till rolls out. But these harmonies are so divergent from the harmonies of what we know, from our own observations and from the history of ethical ideas, as the spiritually and morally sensitive life, that their meaning in the total context of the book offers itself as ironic meaning: the morality that is preached by Moll is a burlesque of morality.

But if Defoe "intended" Moll's little moral sermons as the message of his book (and he does, in his Author's Preface, so guarantee them for us as his own persuasions), how can they be said to be ironic? We are left with two possibilities. Either *Moll Flanders* is a collection of scandal-sheet anecdotes naïvely patched together with the platitudes that form the morality of an impoverished soul (Defoe's), a "sincere" soul but a confused and degraded one; or *Moll Flanders* is a great novel, coherent in structure, unified and given its shape and significance by a complex system of ironies. The most irreducible fact about the book is that we read it—and reread it—with gusto and marvel. We could not do this if it were the former of our alternatives. That it may be the latter is justified by the analysis it yields itself to, as an ironic structure, and most of all justified by our pleasure in it. Shall we, then, waive the question of Defoe's "intention" and "sincerity"? Speculations as to these apparently can add nothing to the book nor can they take anything from it; the book remains what it is. And we do not have appropriate instruments for analysis of Defoe's intention and sincerity, in the deepest meaning of intention and sincerity. We might guess that a great book could not be written by an impoverished soul, and that imponderable traits of moral sensitivity and prophetic intuition might lie in an author and realize themselves in his book without his recognition of them: these would be guesses. Not guess, but inescapable assurance from the quality of the book, is Defoe's understanding of his creature, Moll, whatever else he might not have recognized or understood in the work that was going on under his own hand as the product of his observant eye and his faculty for clean selection and coherent arrangement. In understanding his creature without the slightest divarication from her movements and her thoughts, he gave to Moll the immense and seminal reality of an Earth Mother, progenitrix of the wasteland, sower of our harvests of technological skills, bombs, gadgets, and the platitudes and stereotypes and absurdities of a morality suitable to a wasteland world.

Conscious Irony in *Moll Flanders:*
Facts and Problems

by Maximillian E. Novak

Discussions of irony in *Moll Flanders* are reminiscent of Sir William Petty's famous choice of weapons and site for a duel: axes in a dark cellar. Dorothy Van Ghent has put the problem very neatly. "We are left," she wrote, "with two possibilities. Either *Moll Flanders* is a collection of scandal sheet anecdotes naively patched together with the platitudes that form the morality of an impoverished soul (Defoe's), a 'sincere' soul but a confused and degraded one; or *Moll Flanders* is a great novel, coherent in structure, unified and given its shape and significance by a complex system of ironies." Miss Van Ghent concludes that it must be a great novel because we reread it with delight. "That it may be the latter is justified by the analysis it yields itself to, as an ironic structure, and most of all justified by our pleasure in it. Shall we, then, waive the question of Defoe's 'intention' and 'sincerity'? Speculations as to these apparently can add nothing to the book nor can they take anything from it; the book remains what it is." [1] She adds that we have no way of measuring Defoe's "intention and sincerity, in the deepest meaning of intention and sincerity," and that the question is irrelevant.

Those critics who have doubted that *Moll Flanders* is ironic have suggested that they have some knowledge of this intention and sincerity. In his introduction to the Modern Library edition of *Moll Flanders* Mark Schorer suggested that what appears like irony is merely the result of Defoe's moral confusion—the "classic revelation of the mercantile mind." And in what appears like a devastatingly documented attack, Ian Watt, in *The Rise of the Novel*, claimed that all the evidence points to Defoe's failure to write ironically. More recently, in *To the Palace of Wisdom*, Martin Price has argued that al-

"Conscious Irony in Moll Flanders: *Facts and Problems" by Maximillian E. Novak. From* College English, *26 (December, 1964), 198–204. Reprinted by permission of the National Council of Teachers of English and Maximillian E. Novak.*

[1] [See this volume, pp. 30–39.]

though Defoe seems to have been aware of the moral complexity of his subject matter, he was not being ironic in *Moll Flanders*. All of these writers claim special knowledge of Defoe's background. Schorer appeals to the mercantilist mind; Watt has hooked Defoe up to the Protestant Ethic dynamo of Weber and Tawney; and Martin Price has appealed to Perry Miller and the puritan mind.

In the most current article on this subject, Howard Koonce's "Moll's Muddle: Defoe's Use of Irony in *Moll Flanders*," [2] an essay mercifully free from references to mercantile ethics and puritanism, the critic ably refutes Ian Watt's conclusions and demonstrates that whether we think Defoe's irony is good or bad is a matter for critical judgment but that there is no question that *Moll Flanders* is an ironic novel. But he weakens his point by remarking: "We shall probably never be able to separate with any degree of certainty how much of the irony of *Moll Flanders* is due to conscious authorial effort from how much of it is due to perceptions we bring to rather than get from Defoe." I am in entire agreement with Mr. Koonce and Miss Van Ghent on the irony of *Moll Flanders*, but I cannot see why the areas of irony cannot be established. As Wayne Booth argues in *The Rhetoric of Fiction*, "the question is an important one: if we find ourselves laughing at the author along with his characters, our opinion of the book as art must suffer." I have examined the ironic implications of the first section of *Moll Flanders* in my article on "Moll Flanders' First Love," and in my book *Economics and the Fiction of Daniel Defoe* and will not repeat my conclusions here. What I want to do in this article is to outline some of the general areas of irony which the reader may pick out of *Moll Flanders*, to indicate those themes and elements of human behavior which Defoe regarded as inherently paradoxical and hence subject to ironic treatment, and to assure those readers who have found irony in *Moll Flanders* that Defoe was being consciously ironic.

Of course in order to do this, the critic must have read a good part of the five hundred and forty-seven items which appear in Professor John Robert Moore's *Checklist of the Writings of Daniel Defoe* (Professor Moore has subsequently added several more), but this is precisely what none of the critics appear to have done. Many of these works are long, some are dull, but all of them give us some insight into Defoe's mind. If an appeal to intention may seem a heresy in modern criticism, I can justify myself on the ground that the confusion concerning his irony is a result of appeals to sociological and biographical generalizations about Defoe's puritanism. One would think that the first job of such criticism would be to define Defoe's puritanism, to remember that he was more a contemporary of Swift, Addison, and Steele

---

[2] [See this volume, pp. 49–59.]

than of Milton, Baxter, and Bunyan, and to consider that during the
last thirty years of his life he was a professional writer, not a tradesman.

We should begin by dispelling the idea implied by Professor Watt
that *The Shortest Way with the Dissenters* is Defoe's only other work
of irony. To the contrary, irony was one of his most common modes.
Defoe was not being quite honest in claiming that *The Shortest Way*
was an "irony not unusual." It was very unusual, and his usual method
is much more blatant. More typical of his irony are the blame by
praise techniques employed in his *A Letter to Mr. Bisset* (1709); the
fallacious arguments of *Reasons against the Succession of the House
of Hanover* (1713); and the suspension of moral judgments in *The Life
of Jonathan Wild* (1725). He used the same techniques that appear in
The Shortest Way in a work he must have written at the same time,
King William's Affection to the Church of England Examin'd (1703),
but he broke the illusion of his ironic mask, a fictional opponent of
King William, before the end. *The Shortest Way* was, as Defoe con-
fessed, deliberately intended to fool some people. It was the irony described by Kierkegaard in his paraphrase of Aristotle: an irony which
"tends essentially towards one person" as the extent of its audience.

But let us start with Professor Watt's definition of irony to see how
well Defoe's irony meets his demands. "Irony," writes Professor Watt,
"in its extended sense expresses a deep awareness of the contradictions
and incongruities that beset man in this vale of tears, an awareness
which is manifested in the text's purposeful susceptibility to contradictory interpretations. As soon as we have become aware of the
author's ulterior purpose, we can see all the apparent contradictions
as indications of the coherent attitude underlying the whole work."
Defoe's irony will fit this definition if we make some qualifications.
Defoe saw man's condition in terms of contradictions and incongruities, but he did not always resolve his position on these matters. As Martin Price has very accurately observed, "Like Mandeville, who struts much more in the role, he is one of the artists
who makes our moral judgments more difficult." Secondly, we have to
realize that Defoe regarded irony as a rhetorical trope. The only rhet-
orician whom he quotes is Gerardus Vossius, and it is here that we
must search for clues to Defoe's use of irony. Vossius separates irony
as a way of life, the Socratic manner of dissembling and false humility,
from the rhetorical concept in which "we speak in one way but our
meaning bears no relation to what we literally say." He defines it as a
form of "mockery" by means of "deception and trickery." Quoting
Fabius he notes that irony is understood "either by the tone of voice,
or by the character of the person speaking, or by the situation. For if
any of those is discordant with the words, it is apparent that the meaning of the utterance is the opposite." And finally he warns of the

difficulty of irony: "The circumstances and the rest should be given careful attention if we are to avoid suspecting irony where there is none, or where there is irony, taking the words literally."

If we grant Defoe's familiarity with such a theory we can stop worrying about his naïveté. Moll's words are those of a woman in a state of prosperity and repentance. As a character she tends to be blind to her situation and to reveal only the dimmest understanding of her true moral state. We cannot know her tone of voice, but Defoe will vary his style to suggest sincerity or sophistic rationalization. I want to turn now to consider the various points of incongruity where Defoe's irony may be measured:

1. *Morality:* In his fiction Defoe operated on two levels of morality. The first was a standard Christian morality with charity as the highest of virtues. It is difficult to determine the degree to which the Christianity of the fictions is eccentrically puritan. The second was that connected with natural law. This view sees man as a creature motivated mainly by self: self-love, self-interest, and self-defense. Natural law was codified by Grotius and Pufendorf in the seventeenth century, and Defoe drew upon them for his moral judgments concerning natural behavior. "Natural" is a key word in *Moll Flanders,* and Defoe draws some irony from the disparity between the judgments of the repentant Moll concerning her life passed under the laws of nature. Thus when she says that she was driven by the devil to steal and then excuses herself on the grounds of her poverty, we can see her upbraiding herself for an act which not for a moment could she have avoided. The great virtue of the heroic follower of natural morality is activity, and Moll is one of the most active of his protagonists. Vices include the unnatural: ingratitude, incest, and doing evil to others where there is no excuse to be found in self-preservation or self-interest. It is a moral code which is peculiarly modern in its implications, for it abstracts the individual from specific social institutions and religion and establishes a "natural" standard based on the sophisticated view of human customs which voyagers to foreign lands had made available to the European.

2. *Repentance:* Defoe was not being ironic about Moll's repentance and conversion in Newgate. That we are told in the preface that she is no longer as penitent as she was may make us question some of the attacks upon her natural morality in the name of a more conventional Christian morality, but the conversion and repentance in Newgate follows the pattern of a true repentance which appears in Defoe's other writings. Defoe would have allowed for the possibility that a woman like Moll could repent, and the sincerity of tone in these passages should leave little question about the suspension of irony. Here the repentant narrator is dealing with her greatest moment. The remark in the preface merely suggests that Moll remains true to her essential character—a character which fits ill with a perpetually fervent convert.

3. *Sex, Love, and Marriage:* Defoe once noted that God did not put the sexual instinct under the control of the reason, and in this it differed

from the passions which might be controlled. Sex, then, subjects men and women to a universal comedy in which the main joke lies in the human condition. Thus his most sympathetic hero, Colonel Jacque, is continually cuckolded by his wives, and poor Robin, Moll's first husband, whose defense of marriage for love rather than money Defoe would have found admirable, marries his brother's mistress, who goes to the wedding like "a bear to the stake."

A large part of *Moll Flanders* is devoted to the comedy of sex, love and marriage, and Defoe's sympathies remain divided. He thought that the women were worse off than the men, for they cannot buy a husband if they do not have money, and once they marry, they are at the mercy of their husbands. Defoe's only solution was to advise women to become as capable as men—to educate themselves for survival in a masculine world. Moll's rather masculine nature does not appear until her disillusionment, and, unlike the feminist, Roxana, she always prefers to assume a feminine role. But her ideals should not be confused with Defoe's. Her desire for a "gentleman" husband, who proves useless in the American plantation, is part of the marriage comedy.

Defoe's ideal is one which we can still understand—a marriage for love, a wife who is understanding and helpful, a husband who is a companion and a conscientious provider. Ideally both should be religious and of the same religion. But Defoe seldom presented this ideal and regarded any workable compromise as acceptable. He did not regard polygamy as the worst of sins, for natural law had shown that it was a common institution, and by the same standard of natural law, he regarded desertion as equivalent to divorce. Incest was considered to be contrary to the law of nature, and Moll cannot endure her incestuous marriage to her brother. Even her desire for security must yield to her natural detestation of this relationship.

4. *Children:* The injunctions of natural law state that parents must care for and educate their children, but that in cases of necessity, [they] may give them away. Moll gives love and care where she has the money to afford it. The important point here is that self-preservation was allowed to take precedence over parental love. Defoe seems to have accepted Moll's attitude toward her children as natural enough.

5. *Servants:* After her training with her foster mother, Moll becomes a servant in the home of the Colchester family. She speaks of herself as if she were an adopted daughter, but she is called Miss Betty (the generic name for chamber maids) and is at best a servant-companion to the daughters. Defoe wrote a variety of works attacking the insolence of servants, but he also admired the clever servant who has the ability to rise in the world. Like Mandeville, he knew that the social structure was in flux, but he was much more an exponent of *la carrière ouverte aux talents* than his contemporary. In Moll, then, Defoe illustrates the servant who is not clever enough to trick the heir of the family into marriage but pretty enough to win a younger son. Defoe's attitude toward the young Moll, who dislikes servitude and admires the independence of the town whore, is detached, amused, critical, and ironic. The irony of the first part of

the book which ends with the death of Robin is perfectly clear and free from the complications of more serious themes—the possibility of starvation and destitution.

6. *Poverty (Necessity)*: When a person falls into a state of destitution which makes starvation a possibility, he may do anything to preserve his life. Some writers on natural law believed that such a state dissolved the bonds of society and made all goods common. Defoe placed the following limitations on man's freedom when confronted by this "first and great principle of nature": (a) He must not harm someone in the same condition as himself (a condition of equal poverty or danger). (b) He must try to make restitution of whatever he steals or repair whatever harm he has done when it is possible. (c) His degree of guilt depends to some extent on the degree to which he is to blame for falling into a state of necessity. When Moll blames herself for her crimes she judges herself from a standpoint of divine law and excuses herself on grounds of natural law. The paradox lies in the limitations of the human condition. She condemns herself for her failure to resist temptation, but then argues that human nature is too frail to resist the laws of nature.

7. *Positive Law:* Even Coke argued that no national law could overrule the laws of nature or the laws of God. Such laws could not be regarded as valid. But Moll lives in a society which will punish her for violating its laws. English law tells her that she cannot steal no matter how hungry she is, and she cannot remarry while her husband is alive. Moll always follows the laws of nature, but the contrasts between the three levels of law are responsible for much of the paradoxical morality in *Moll Flanders* and in Defoe's other works.

8. *Thieves and Tradesmen:* Defoe frequently contrasted the honesty of the thief who will steal through necessity and the dishonesty of the grasping tradesman. He suggested that the worst pirates were more honest than the capitalists of his time and superior in every way to the directors of the South Sea Company. He even suggests that Jonathan Wild destroyed honor among thieves when he organized them as an industrialist. Defoe blamed theft and piracy upon the laws of England and English society with its unfair treatment of debtors, its failure to care for the poor, and its ill treatment of seamen. But he also recognized that a society must punish crime or fall into anarchy.

9. *Prostitutes:* Defoe attacked Mandeville's suggestion concerning legalizing prostitution, but he objected to the manner rather than the matter. Defoe sympathized with the prostitute and argued that she does not support society by consuming its goods (as Mandeville suggested) and that her life is miserable, for he did not believe that she experienced any sexual pleasure in her job. In sketching the decline of women into prostitution he argued that the primary guilt lay with the man who first seduced her. Moll is hardly reluctant but the rake who seduces her is still more at fault.

10. *Gentlemen:* Moll has affairs with three "gentlemen." The first robs her of her virtue and refuses to marry her. The second is a "gentleman-tradesman," who spends all her money and leaves her destitute. The third is a "gentleman-highwayman" who tries to cheat her but proves to be a loving

spouse. All of these men have in common an aspiration to a life of leisure. Moll's aspiration toward gentility and her disapproval of her Lancashire Husband's idleness in America suggests an appropriate "muddle" in Moll's mind which is hardly in Defoe's. Defoe frequently attacked those rakish gentlemen who added nothing to the wealth of the society and were a plague to the women. The Lancashire Husband is the best of the group both because he reveals a good heart and because he led an active life of crime to support himself.

11. *Economic Individualism:* Defoe was fully aware of the movement in feeling and ideas which Tawney and Weber described and stood staunchly against it in the name of older mercantilist ideals. He was continually proposing state intervention in trade, the establishment of cooperative communities and societies from orphanages to homes for the aged. In 1704 he complained that "it is now almost become a Maxim with them [Dissenting ministers], that poverty proceeds from want of Grace, Inverting the Scriptures. That only with [rich?] Men, can enter the Kingdom of Heaven, at least into their Congregation." Though he dramatized the struggle for wealth in his fiction, Defoe's ideal was always that of retirement when a moderate wealth was achieved. There may appear to be a paradox in his admiration for both activity and retirement, but Defoe did not insist that the activity had to be economic. Colonel Jacque seeks gentility and an education after he has gained wealth.

12. *Projects:* Defoe has Moll remind the reader that some nations have hospitals to take care of orphans and much time is spent on the home for expectant mothers operated by the woman who later becomes her "Governess." These are both ideas which Defoe is advancing with some seriousness, but in both cases he uses them dramatically. Moll is given what ought to be a perfectly good training for servitude by the parish. Her inability to accept servitude has something to do with heredity (she sucked her mother's milk in Newgate) and something to do with environment (she was raised by gypsies until the age of three). She should have been spared both experiences and trained more thoroughly. The Governess has some excellent ideas, but Defoe would have disapproved of her sly suggestion about abortion; and we are not surprised to find that the establishment slips into evil ways.

13. *Colonial Propaganda:* Defoe presents the possibility of a new life in America for the transported criminal in both his fiction and didactic works. He believed that the criminal might become a wealthy property owner through hard work and ingenuity. Though Jacque feels that he needs the official status of an army officer, education, and travel before he can regard himself as a gentleman, Defoe recognized the relativity of status in such a society.

It should be clear from this summary of themes in *Moll Flanders* that the underlying irony of the work is to be found in Moll's blindness or, as Mr. Koonce calls it, her "muddle." The fog that I wish to dispel is that which hangs over Defoe's puritanism and moral insensitivity. Defoe's sophisticated attitude toward human nature as governed by natural law allowed him to see mankind free from the claims of religion and social customs. His training in economics enabled him to dramatize some of the most fascinating sociological currents of his day. On the surface level of her narrative Moll sees her life as a Christian penitent. She is only dimly aware that she operates on a level of natural law, pursuing security through marriage and then self-preservation through theft. One is reminded of Marvin Mudrick's comment on Jane Austen's *Emma* when that peculiarly obtuse heroine repents her deeds: "the act of self-abasement that claims sin, in order to avoid the responsibility of self-knowledge." Moll never understands why she does not stop stealing after she has enough money to live on, but Defoe allows us to see the pleasure which she takes in her craft. We see her self-satisfaction; we never see her self-recognition. Mr. Koonce suggests that to a certain extent Moll's blindness is our blindness. Whereas Roxana has Amy to talk with and to reveal herself to, Moll presents us with a closed world. Her husbands reveal little about her and her Governess seems to be merely a reflection of her wishes. Like many people, she sees the world through her rationalizations and pretensions, and though we can see where these are grossly false, we can only guess at the rest. I would repeat the suggestion which I made elsewhere that we take the suggestion in the preface of a trilogy centered on Moll, her Lancashire Husband, and the Governess more seriously. Defoe usually wrote in clusters. *Robinson Crusoe* became a trilogy and both *Captain Singleton* and *Colonel Jacque* grew out of earlier works; there are two lives of Sheppard, two of Wild, and his works on magic and the devil grew to three volumes. The preface suggests that the two other accounts of Moll give a different view of her personality, and it is possible that Defoe was saving some of his material for other volumes.

Nevertheless what we have satisfies Miss Van Ghent's analysis of a "complex system of ironies." As for Professor Watt's doubts about Defoe's capacity for handling the rhetoric of irony, I would suggest that Defoe's training in rhetoric at the Newington Green Academy was very thorough. In his *Compleat English Gentleman* Defoe described how Charles Morton taught his students to imitate the style of various characters: "Some times they were Ministers of State, Secretaries and Commissioners at home, and wrote orders and instructions to the ministers abroad, as by order of the King in Council and the like. Thus he taught his pupils to write a masculine and manly stile, to write the most polite English, and at the same time to kno' how to suit their manner as well to the subject they were to write upon as to the person or degrees of persons they were to write to." It is clear that Defoe learned his lessons well in this "class for eloquence."

That his readers frequently did not understand his irony is possible, but if this is true, we may wonder why he continued to employ irony in his writings throughout his life. And was Defoe's audience very different from Swift's? The very realism of his fiction was considered "low" and put it outside the pale of polite literature during his day. But there is no reason to believe that it was not read and understood. Professor Watt has raised some valuable questions; our answers to these problems should begin with the unquestionable fact that *Moll Flanders* is a work of irony.

Moll's Muddle: Defoe's Use
of Irony in *Moll Flanders*

by Howard L. Koonce

Because the careful work of such men as Dottin and Secord has left
us no room to doubt that we are dealing with a far more important
achievement than the skilful transcription of fact which has long been
allowed, the most important critical question about Defoe has become
that of artistic control. And perhaps the most impressive, certainly the
most provocative, response to this question has been by Ian Watt, who
asserts that realistic prose fiction had to unify the forces of theme,
character, and moral concern to become art, and who finds that the
incongruities and inconsistencies of Defoe's work in general, and of
Moll Flanders in particular, fail to coalesce into any such structural
unity.[1] This carefully documented point of view provides a useful check
to the overenthusiastic response of novelists like Virginia Woolf and
critics like Dorothy Van Ghent. Watt warns that what we have taken
to be ironic masterstrokes are very often perceptions we bring to rather
than get from Defoe. And he shows us that such incongruities as that
which Mrs. Van Ghent has noticed between "a lusty, full-bodied, lively-
sensed creature" and the "astounding" unimportance of sensuous life
in Moll's world could just as possibly result from a real lack of the
tactile sense in Moll, if not in Defoe as well, as it could from the
intricate world of interlaced ironies Mrs. Van Ghent rhapsodizes about.[2]

Yet when Professor Watt asserts that there is no ironic structure of
any kind, that "whatever disagreement there may be about particular
instances, it is surely certain that there is no consistently ironical attitude present in *Moll Flanders*," surely he is wrong. For it still seems
evident to me that this is a work of comic excellence because it is

From "Moll's Muddle: Defoe's Use of Irony in Moll Flanders*" by Howard L.
Koonce. From ELH, 30, no. 4 (1963), 277–88, 390–91. Copyright © 1963 by The Johns
Hopkins Press. Reprinted by permission of The Johns Hopkins Press.*

[1] Ian Watt, *The Rise of the Novel* (Berkeley and Los Angeles, 1957), hereafter
cited as Watt. [See this volume, pp. 17–29.]

[2] In *The English Novel, Form and Function* (New York, 1953), p. 35. [See this
volume, pp. 30–39.]

basically ironic in structure, even though it has not come to entirely
satisfactory terms with the episodic nature of the narrative of its time.

Professor Watt contends that the "moral imperceptiveness which is
so laughably clear to us is in fact a reflection of one of the psychological
characteristics of Puritanism which Defoe shared with his heroine."
On the strength of a study of moral outbursts in *Commonwealth*
pamphlets, but without citing any instances of such pamphleteering by
Defoe, he says that the Puritan was "much more addicted to outbursts
of moral indignation than were the Royalists," and that he had "a
complementary tendency . . . to be mercifully blind to his own faults."
And then he cites this much of the famous episode in which Moll steals
a necklace from a child:

> I only thought I had given the parents a just reproof for their negligence,
> in leaving the poor lamb to come home by itself, and it would teach them
> to take more care another time.

About it, he says: "There is no doubt about the psychological veracity
of the reflection: the conscience is a great casuist. There is, however,
some doubt about Defoe's intention: is it meant to be an ironical
touch about his heroine's moral duplicities, her tendency to be blind
to the beam in her own eye? or did Defoe forget Moll as he raged
inwardly at the thought of how careless parents are, and how richly
they deserve to be punished?" Now it seems to me that Professor Watt
has missed almost every point, ostensible as well as underlying, that
the passage has to make in his oversimplified set of alternatives.

The passage, in context, makes it quite clear that Moll is not only
not "blind to the beam in her own eye," but that she is actually be-
rating herself for it. Immediately before the quotation Watt selects, she
says: "poverty, as I have said, hardened my heart, and my own neces-
sities made me regardless of anything." And though she does accuse
parents and maid of vanity and carelessness, there is nothing in the
language of the passage even remotely suggestive of rage. More important, however, far from forgetting Moll, Defoe is here depicting her in
her most characteristic activity. She is ingratiating and exculpating
herself by wandering into a thoroughly disarming moral muddle. And
it seems to me that Defoe was not only aware of this muddle, but that
he in fact planned and executed it as a means of uniting what had long
been the two basic elements of the criminal narrative.

The basic elements of Moll's muddle are quite obviously a zest for
tales of criminal ingenuity and a taste for moral preachment. The incongruities caused by Defoe's combination of these elements, of course,
create the possibility of irony. Now despite Professor Watt's belief that
the revelation of these incongruities comes about because of "the

searching power of formal realism, which permits and indeed encourages the presentation of literary objects and attitudes which had not hitherto jostled each other in the same work," the moral and criminal objects and attitudes basic to *Moll Flanders* had been jostling each other in single works at least as early as the Mary Carleton Narratives of 1663–1673.[3] Here is a sample from Francis Kirkman's version of the story. Moll Carleton has just lifted a goldsmith's bill from the gentleman keeping her, and has invented a wild goose chase to get him out of bed and gone:

> He . . . soon rises, and taking leave of her begins his journey. No sooner was he gone, but she makes ready for hers; and, being dressed, she takes coach for the goldsmith's. When she was almost come thither, she drew out the bill to look on it. And it was well she did so, or else all her project would have been spoiled, for she intended to demand a just hundred pound, when, looking on the backside of the bill, she found that twenty pound of the hundred had been received. This startled her, and troubled her to think that she was twenty pound worse than she thought for. . . .
>
> She, being now come to the goldsmith's shop, told him that she came from such a gentleman, who had such a day left a hundred pound, but had received twenty pound; and he, being sick, had sent her for the eighty remaining. . . .
>
> She, being now the mistress of this rich cargo of eighty pound in money, the jewel of fifty pound which he had given her, and several other rings, pendants, and necklaces to a good value, was resolved to march off, leave her old friend, and seek a new, or at leastwise new quarters. But she was much disturbed and vexed that she was disappointed twenty pound in her expectation, and thought how she might make that good. . . . She therefore returned to her lodging, and, not having the keys, breaks open the locks of a trunk and box, and rifles them both, where she finds twenty pieces of old gold, a golden seal, an old watch, and some odd pieces of plate. . . .
>
> And now I have related this story of her, is she not a bad ungrateful woman thus to leave a man who so handsomely provided for her? Had it not been better for her to have continued with him, who loved, tendered, and would always have taken care of her, and kept her from running into those lewd courses that she since then committed? Was it not enough for her to take the gentleman's bill. . . . Well, let her go for a base lewd woman! But time will come that she must repent this unhandsome, ingrateful action. And thus you see how dearly this man paid for her wanton company. If he had any music, he paid the fiddler soundly, or she

[3] Ernest Bernbaum, *The Mary Carleton Narratives 1663–1673* (Cambridge, Mass., 1914) studies these works. Many of the texts he refers to have been reprinted by Spiro Peterson in *"The Counterfeit Lady Unveiled" and Other Criminal Fictions of Seventeenth-Century England* (Garden City, N. Y., 1961).

paid herself; his sweet meat cost him sour sauce, and so will hers in the end.

But she had much more work cut out for her to do. . . .[4]

Here are not only most of the elements of formal realism,[5] here if anywhere is to be located Watt's distinction between an "ironic object" and a "work of irony," the former being an object produced by incongruous attitudes and objects accidentally jostling each other. Not that there is any doubt about which side Kirkman is on. But it is here that the very attention to detail which formal realism "permits and indeed encourages" confesses the simultaneous fascination with and revulsion from criminal ingenuity Professor Watt thinks characteristic of the Puritan mind. And though *Moll Flanders,* too, is basically involved with this paradoxical attitude, it is in Kirkman's piece that one of the elements of the paradox is merely inconsistent with the other. For Defoe made of these elements the basic conflict of his work by projecting and sustaining, in incident and in structure, the consistent, life-like muddle of a woman with a powerful, unmotivated sense of manifest destiny which she is in the act of reconciling with an equally powerful, if conveniently underdeveloped, sense of morality.

Making use of the obvious fact that any tale of the past is always to be considered an inseparable compound of past actions and present attitudes, Defoe, it seems to me, wrote a book about his heroine's consciousness of her career in relation to her consciousness of right and wrong, both rendered at the time of telling.[6] The main action of this book I take to be what Moll considers a repentant confession, but what is quite obviously an amazingly self-confident appeal for sympathy. Old Moll has achieved the entire position she "innocently" set out to achieve long before in Colchester. And she is now presenting her story, as a genuine confession, to those who, like her, have a decent kind of traditional morality, equipped with such things as an appropriate concern for chastity, a horror of incest, and a revulsion from theft—

---

[4] Bernbaum, pp. 72–74.

[5] Bernbaum, p. 90, summarizes the common characteristics he found in the techniques of Kirkman and Defoe: "The serious moral tone, the minute depiction of occurrences, the coherence of the plot, the tracing of the motives of the characters, and the elaborate creation of verisimilitude,—those qualities, whose combination is usually considered original with Defoe, we have seen to be prevailing traits of 'The Counterfeit Lady.'"

[6] Watt . . . sees Defoe's "failure" to use the double time scheme implicit in the first-person narrative as one proof of his lack of structural skill. Certainly it did become conventional in the novel to keep the time of telling and the time of occurrence separate. But this is pretty surely an artifice rather than an imitation of the normal workings of the mind. And to try Defoe on the basis of a convention which developed later is to display quite as anachronistic a reading as any of those Professor Watt points a finger at.

and yet who have enough awareness of the world to know what poverty can lead a person to.

It is because this appeal for sympathy is perfectly regular, is based on a perfectly consistent pattern, that we find Moll Flanders herself a consistent human being regardless of her mercurial attitudes towards other matters. If, that is to say, we were to try to figure out what Moll's basic attitude towards her children really *was*, we would only wander about in a maze of reactions extending from her splenetic dismissal of those she got in Colchester to her rapturous exclamations and actions in Virginia over a son born of repulsive incest. But if we ask what her attitude *is*, we can quite confidently consider her children as we can everything and everybody else in the book, a means for turning the trick of sympathy, episode by episode. And to turn this trick for a woman who robbed children in parks and could even conceive of killing one of them, to turn it not only without the self-flagellating flail but with a kind of pride of accomplishment was indeed ambition.

In accomplishing such a line of action, Defoe was able to both elevate and bring into real contact the old criminal and moral interests of this type of narrative. He could retain the same kind of moralizing commentary as Kirkman's but without direct, authorial intervention. And more important, barring but really vicious acts, he was able to free the old fascination with criminal ingenuity from the all too vehement suppression of *exemplum* tales like Kirkman's and give it a validity of its own. This he did by creating a character profoundly superior to her environment, by endowing her with a simple, really unconscious sensitivity to the discrepancy, and then by supplying a kind of malignant fate to keep her from achieving her proper destiny by any other than criminal means. Thus, Defoe provided a double source of tension for his work. Moll's sense of destiny not only was in conflict with her circumstances, it is in conflict with her own sense of morality; the book is a series of interlocking challenges to Moll's ingenuity and resourcefulness not only in overcoming adversity, but also in turning grossly culpable behavior into a matter for admiration or sympathy or both.

So, like most of the episodes in *The Counterfeit Lady*, all except a very few of the episodes in *Moll Flanders* are built on a basic pattern which combines a tale of criminal ingenuity—or at least illegal or reprehensible ingenuity—with moralizing commentary. But what emerges from this combination in Defoe is not at all a self-conscious *exemplum* transcribed from writers like Kirkman. Instead, in very nearly the same breath she uses to vividly portray the culpable act, Moll accuses herself of wrong-doing. Then, she wanders into her characteristic, often preposterously heightened moral muddle in which the deed is rendered harmless. And in the process, by means of one or more of the following methods, her guilt is acknowledged only to be diverted so that the unacknowledged spring of her destiny is allowed room for another movement.

Most frequently, Moll simply pleads necessity, meaning by the word a real or apprehended threat to physical existence.[7] Sometimes she takes care to separate herself from gross villainy, as she does when she leaves the Mint or when she insistently labels the criminals below decks "they" while she is being transported. More often, she uses other characters either to demonstrate her own innate goodness under assault by circumstances beyond her control (e.g., the long debate with her Governess about a foster home for her illegitimate child, or to distribute blame to such an extent that her own act is swallowed up in a world of villainy, as she does when she submits and marries the younger brother at Colchester. And on some occasions, such as the one cited below, she even makes long and tenuous digressions when nothing else will serve.

And despite the fact that Moll considers her salvation to have begun in Newgate and that she seems to feel she is satisfying her moral sense in the very process of consolidating the status she was moved towards so long ago in Colchester, she remains aware of the conflicting claims which her appeal for sympathy occasions as long as there is a story to tell. When, for instance, Moll becomes aware that the necessity to conceal the circumstances of her former married life in Virginia for financial reasons is in conflict with her duty to be open with her husband, she promptly and typically stops the narrative for a moral dissertation. The theme of this one concerns the problem of keeping secrets; yet she illustrates it with the almost completely irrelevant tale of the night-flying prisoner, released to steal because he would tell all the circumstances in his sleep and his keepers could then return the stolen goods for a reward. Nevertheless, behaving with superb self-confidence, Moll then addresses the reader directly to prove that she is really an honest, open woman obeying both larger moral impulses and nature:

> As the publishing this account of my life is for the sake of the just moral of every part of it, and for instruction, caution, warning, and improvement to every reader, so this will not pass, I hope, for an unnecessary digression concerning some people being obliged to disclose the greatest secrets either of their own or other people's affairs.

Having thus completely befuddled the moral claim which started the whole thing, she can go on:

---

[7] Maximillian E. Novak, in his "The Problem of Necessity in Defoe's Fiction," *PQ*, XL (1961), 513–24, has carefully documented both the fact of Defoe's conscious concern with and general position in regard to the meaning of the term.

> Under the certain oppression of this weight upon my mind, I laboured in the case I have been naming; and the only relief I found for it was to let my husband into so much of it as I thought would convince him of the necessity there was for us to think of settling in some other part of the world; and the next consideration before us was. . . .

It is when no more of these conflicts seem impending that the book stops.

In this way projecting Moll's muddle in the incidents of the story, and thereby putting into real conflict the old interests of the criminal narrative, Defoe sustained it by means of a similar kind of conflict in the structure of the book. For Moll's consciousness of the structure of her story is at odds with its real form.

Actually, Moll's story is the series of episodic variations on the theme of resourcefulness which is outlined above. Though both her physical resources and the objects she pits them against change, the series shows no development at all either in her essential outlook or her skill in handling the situations which confront her. It is on this structural level that Moll is clearly revealed as an already fully developed character, reconciling the morally illicit events of her past with her sense of morality in a bid for the reader's sympathy.

In Moll's consciousness, however, her story has all the structure of traditional Christian experience. Her life is to her a kind of journey to salvation, the history of a woman who lost what she calls her virtue and her modesty and so, as she says, "had nothing of value left to recommend me, either to God's blessing or man's assistance." Thus left to her own devices, she compounded her sins to and beyond the extent indicated by the sub-title of the book. And finally caught, she learned the fear of God in Newgate, repented, reformed, and became the penitent, confronted with a wicked past, who is revealing it for the reader's benefit. On this structural level, Moll is satisfied that she has become a completely changed character, that she has worked out a resolution of the conflict within her, her warring impulses come to rest together in a landed state of penitence.

But by setting this apparent movement of the story at odds with the static, non-developing series of episodes, Defoe in fact maintained the muddle, and we recognize Moll's resolution to be an absurd, preposterous logical triumph, in which her sense of morality has been completely absorbed into her sense of destiny, the conventional values she professes completely redefined and made subservient to economic success, the moral value she is convinced her narrative has by way of example unequivocally inverted to entirely the opposite effect.

In the light of Professor Watt's contention that we of the twentieth century get the irony Defoe could not because of our enlightened view

of economic self-interest and "protestations of piety," it cannot be em-
phasized too much that Moll is confessing—that she professes awareness
of her own wrong-doing. She is fully aware, for instance, that she com-
mits a sin of her own in letting the elder brother of Colchester go. But,
she says, "he reasoned me out of my reason." The point of irony arises
not because Moll is making "pious protestations" or making a Puritan-
ical attack on the wrong-doing of others while overlooking her own,
but because she seems to be psychologically unaffected by her awareness of her own wrong-doing, because she does not stop for self-flagel-
lation. Instead, she plunges on with diction which confesses the complete lack of any such psychological effect:

> I had a great many *adventures* after this, but I was young in the *business*,
> and did not know how to manage, otherwise than as the devil put things
> into my head; and indeed he was seldom backward to me. One *adventure*
> I had which was *very lucky to me*. . . .

Now of this phenomenon, the writer of the "Author's Preface" seems
to be at least mildly aware. He tells of cleaning up a piece "written
more like one still in Newgate than one grown penitent and humble,
as she afterwards *pretends to be*." Or again, speaking of the end of her
life:

> But her husband's life, being written by a third hand, gives a full account
> of them both, how long they lived together in that country, and how
> they both came to England again, after about eight years, in which time
> they were grown very rich, and where she lived, it seems, to be very old,
> *but was not so extraordinary a penitent as she was at first; it seems only
> that indeed she always spoke with abhorrence of her former life,* and of
> every part of it.

Thus, the writer of the preface which includes the promise that
"there is not a superlative villain brought upon the stage, but he is
brought to an unhappy end, or brought to be a penitent" feels obliged
to hedge on that promise in the same preface. And this means, I think,
that neither we nor Defoe can conceive of any such eventuality as Moll
in a static state of self-reproach without thinking her out of existence.
In prison, faced with the death sentence, Moll came to the conclusion
that it was "the greatest stupidity in nature to lay any weight on anything, though the most valuable in the world." But just as her response
to learning of the reprieve from the death sentence which caused these
remarks was even then wholly predictable: "however, I had this
mercy, that I had more time given me, and that it was my business
to improve that time," her achieved state of penitence at the end of
the work is, we know, wholly interchangeable with the state of her
fortune. To Moll, penitence is an activity to be indulged in only when
there is either no necessity or no opportunity "to improve the time."

And though at the end of the book Moll has the opportunity, just as in prison she felt the necessity, to think of asking God's mercy, we are quite sure, and the writer of the preface seems to be aware, that the only real subjects for Moll's thought processes are rather more mundane.

And all of this is to say that Moll exists for us only in moments of active conflict. On the immediate level, it is a conflict between her resourcefulness and a series of circumstances resisting her ability to use it. But on another level, it is a conflict between Moll's awareness of a need for moral and spiritual sanction and the obvious delight she has in telling about, as well as the delight she had in performing, her highly successful manipulation of a series of adverse circumstances. And this level is ironic because that manipulation could satisfy her peculiar sense of necessity only by violating her own spiritual and moral sense of responsibility. It is in this way that Moll has to be considered an artistic creation, not a reportorial offering of a chunk of life. She was created out of a thematic conflict and so controlled that imagining her under any other circumstances at any time is plainly impossible. Hence, though it may be a novelistic fault in the current historical and psychological dogmas of criticism to merely omit any account of the five years she spent outside that conflict with her banker husband, or to say as little about her shorter term with the younger brother of Colchester, all such static situations are plainly irrelevant to the theme of *Moll Flanders*. "The one impossible event," says Virginia Woolf about Moll, "is that she should settle down in comfort and security." [8] . . .

Perhaps the most important part of the characteristic pattern Moll uses in exculpating herself from her past is her claim that necessity drove her to actions her innate sense of goodness would never have allowed, even though she does acknowledge inclination as a kind of secondary force. But Defoe does not allow us to think any such thing. [9]

When Moll uses the word necessity, she means a physical threat to simple survival:

> I had the terrible prospect of poverty and starving, which lay on me as a frightful spectre, so that there was no looking behind me. But as poverty brought me into it, so fear of poverty kept me in it.

[8] "Defoe," in *The Common Reader* (London, 1925), p. 125. [See this volume, pp. 11–16.]

[9] Maximillian Novak assembles an impressive range of evidence to demonstrate the fact that Defoe deliberately used the problem of necessity to pass indirect judgment on the actions of characters in nearly all of his books. Looking at her actions against those of Colonel Jack in comparable situations, he finds that "Moll's guilt is greater than Jack's because although she realizes the extent of her crimes, she refuses either to make restitution or abandon her way of life" (*op. cit.*, p. 522).

On this occasion, that of rationalizing her life with her lover of Bath, poverty kept her in it for six years, at the end of which time she was worth £550, some plate, and a good stock of clothes and linen. And the poverty that brought her into it was the "between two or three hundred pounds" she had been able to salvage out of the considerable sum she brought out of Virginia. There is, in fact, an almost ritualistic stock-taking at the end of every episode in the book.[10] And Moll is never allowed to descend to anything like missing a meal, let alone starvation.

Though she is not at any time aware of it, the concept which Moll's "necessity" as well as her "inclination" represents has a clear referent in the text, one more and more underscored as the book progresses. It is part of the same thing as her apparently motiveless yet nearly hysterical fear of going to service which we hear early in the book, part of the same thing as her consciousness, later, that her mission is "to improve the time" rather than accept an ability to adjust to bad situations. Her "necessity" is really the sense of manifest destiny which I have insisted on above. And Defoe takes care never to let the concept mean anything else. . . .

All these are, I think, clear indications that an attitude other than Moll's is operating in the book. They and many more like them— allowing Moll to exculpate herself by means of the very same reasons she uses to condemn the elder brother at Colchester, for instance— indicate an attitude that can be considered unintentional only at the cost of considering Defoe incredibly obtuse. And they indicate an attitude which was, on one level at least, that of any good reader today. On the one hand, we have a character compelled towards self-realization and able to act in a series of situations where real spiritual and moral awareness would be paralyzing. And on the other, we have that character's compulsion towards a moral and spiritual respectability which needs that awareness to be valid. It is the juxtaposition of these two forces that creates the real and sustaining conflict of the piece. And it is this conflict that Defoe resolves into the delightful muddle of Moll Flanders.

Thus, if the technique of irony means the technique of presenting a consistent but oblique point of view, *Moll Flanders* cannot be called anything but a work of irony. The basic contradiction of its structure,

---

[10] Except one. Just before Moll turns to a life of crime, still without having fore-gone a single meal, however, she pictures her plight as so desperate that it must be the work of the devil himself. It is true, of course, that she is aware that she does not face imminent starvation, "spending upon the main stock" being rather "a certain kind of bleeding to death." But surely the game is given away when we are informed that she thought she could easily live in Manchester on fifteen pounds a year, when she admits, in the middle of her career as a thief, that she could make a living with her needle, and when she is amazed that a shop-girl who earns three pounds a year can turn down a bribe.

the apparent movement from complicity to sin to repentance belied by the static theme and variations on resourcefulness, is the basic contradiction within a narrator unaware of it. And it is not too much to suppose that the separate point of view that sees her muddled is well within Defoe's sense of whimsy, even if much of that muddle was his own. Defoe's success in creating a compelling character out of the incongruous forces conflicting within her is, at least, what novelists like John Peale Bishop mean when they characterize the work as ironic:

> It is in the disparity between what was meant and what was actually achieved that there is scope for the novelist's irony, and without irony the novel has neither conviction or force. That is why obvious virtue is so dull in the novel; a good person who goes straight toward good deeds always fails to convince us, not because goodness does not exist, but because in such a case the novelist has no means of granting it a third dimension.[11]

And a third dimension is specifically what is consciously and artistically offered us by Defoe.

But to demonstrate the point that *Moll* is basically ironic in structure is not to assert that it is a fully satisfactory work of art. Formally, perhaps, we may feel that there is too much essential redundancy in the book, that the development and force of the contrasting thematic structure is stunted undesirably in so repetitive an episodic structure. More important than this, however, though we can be sure that Defoe was aware of and delighted with Moll's muddle, we can have no confidence that he was in full command of its implications to us. It is by trying to fix the limits of the third dimension Defoe offers us, by trying to understand Defoe's ultimate attitude towards the values caught in the thematic muddle of Moll and so to reach our own, that we realize the sharp limitations of the work.

[11] "Moll Flanders' Way," *The Collected Essays of John Peale Bishop*, ed. Edmund Wilson (New York and London, 1948), p. 54.

Preface to *Moll Flanders*

by Cesare Pavese

The Fortunes and Misfortunes of the Famous Moll Flanders was written by Daniel Defoe in his sixties, in the third of those extraordinary six years (1719–24) in which he gave to the world, besides various pamphlets and tracts and biographies, *The Life and Strange Surprizing Adventures of Robinson Crusoe, The Adventures of Captain Singleton, A Journal of the Plague Year, The History and Remarkable Life of Colonel Jacque,* and *Roxana.* Such a luxuriance of creative energy came after an entire existence resolutely spent in the struggles of commercial enterprises, all different and all unsuccessful, and later, when he turned to politics and literature, tested by persecutions, imprisonments, exhausting labors at the writing desk, and above all, poverty.

Nothing can render the temper of this man better than the frank and vigorous voices of his protagonists. They are all alike and the adventure of all is the same: whether children of rich merchants or poor orphans of the prison, they all face a life in which the harshness of their daily plight is equaled only by their tireless resolution; and the repeated and almost biblical desolations in which they are found naked and alone before the world and God take on the shape of tragic pauses from which their energy will emerge intact and even increased. These individuals are essentially alone. In this sense the wearisome solitude of Robinson Crusoe on the island is the most conspicuous and memorable myth of the solitude of each one.

The daily struggle of these people is not concerned with spiritual problems or with protoromantic ideals of passion. Defoe has reduced to its most elementary form the tragedy of existence: "Give us this day our daily bread" is clearly the most insistent prayer that arises from every page of these autobiographies. It is less true that they also pray: "Lead us not into temptation"; or, at least, the genuine piety that gushes from these hearts after the most tremendous trials is only a

---

quite human reflection of their need for security and material suffi-
ciency.

These general considerations will seem no great novelty to Italian
readers of *Robinson Crusoe* and *Captain Singleton*. But it seemed to
me that I ought to recall them in presenting this first Italian translation of the life of Moll Flanders, because they will serve to put in
relief the singularity of tone which I think Defoe has been able this
time to impose upon his usual adventure of struggle, of sin, and of
repentance. I mean this: the figure of Moll Flanders who, through the
richness of her experiences, seems to me the most complex of all the
characters the author has imagined, reveals in the precise and merciless
calmness of her memories a capacity for irony which at times goes well
beyond the obligatory compunction of the penitent. This capacity—be
it said in passing—seems to me to detach Moll Flanders from the whole
varicolored family of heroes of the eighteenth-century novel who always
run to the extremes either of the generic or the characteristic. Above
all, Moll judges herself in contact with a world which the national taste
for sentimentality and humor has not yet managed to deform and
impoverish. Here the autobiographical form, chosen by Defoe perhaps
for mere contingent reasons of literary custom, reveals a more profound
poetic reason. Moll Flanders, and through her the author, feels toward
none of the events or persons she falls in with—and so much the less
toward herself—that witty and idle interest which schematizes reality
in adventures and caricatures, even if these be called Tom Jones. Moll
Flanders doesn't pause to jot down, amused and disturbed, characteristic words or gestures, but from each individual she gathers the essential
significance incarnated in the real sorrow or the real joy which she has
received from them. Especially, she treats herself in this way.

Now this attentive investigation of one's own motives and those of
others, expressed with the implacable awareness of one who is accus-
tomed to conclude the most desperate examinations of conscience with
the detailed accounting in pounds sterling of her remaining means, is
precisely what I call the irony of *Moll Flanders*. It is in the intermingling and in the fusion of these extreme motives that I think this
irony consists. There is much to learn, Moll warns, from my trespasses
and from my repentance: how the most solemn resolutions of virtue
are in vain without the divine support, and "by what methods innocent
people are drawn in, plundered and robbed, and by consequence how
to avoid them." Let's perform our penance, the humble sinner seems
to say, but let's keep our eyes open, because in the end God helps those
who help themselves. In this respect, the most delightful pages are those
of the final years in Virginia, where the favor of Heaven tangibly
blesses, to the clink of sterling, the sage discretion of the wife of
the two husbands. So that it is not then entirely clear if "Mistress

Moll" owes her prosperous and serene old age more to the benevolence of Heaven than to the capacity, of which her existence is a very clear example, of concealing skeletons in the closet.

But I don't want to insist too much on this point lest I create the impression that the attractive Moll is an abstract and inhuman type of "Machiavellian" calculator, an impression which would, among other things, deprive her most unusual voice of all interest and resonance. She, and with her the author, takes life too seriously to be reduced to so superficial a scheme. Let the attentive reader notice— if I have succeeded in preserving in this translation the humble and severe vigor of this most modern of the eighteenth-century English prose styles—all the rich gamut of tones in which these memories live again, from the ribald pages of advice for women in a hurry to get married to those penetrating and dreadful pages on the stay in Newgate and on her own death sentence. Even if there were nothing else, the open and sincere capacity for abandon of which she gives evidence in her adventure with the Lancashire husband would be enough to acquit Moll. To hear her, her whole existence has been one single aspiration for honesty, nor would she ever have been induced to evil if not constrained by the cruelest of needs. In this connection, the periods of time, which she usually dispatches with a few sentences, of her successive married lives, are revelatory, when, a minimum of security and comfort being given her, she becomes the most compunctious of Christians and the most reasonable of wives. It is however true that these periods pass through her memory like lightning, and that there succeed, detailed and implacable, her sorties and robberies against mankind. Well, and so what? She writes so that he who reads can find some instruction, if he would be pleased to treasure it up, and her whole experience keeps telling her that the most generous resolutions and the exercise of the most incontestable virtues irremediably disappear with the last pound sterling. All her life is thus spent in the presence of "the rainy day." And since no one will want to deny that she has plenty of rainy days, we will do well to grant her that initial sympathy of which we all have need.

A Bourgeois Picaroon

by Robert Alter

It is scarcely surprising to discover that a woman who makes a trade out of love can be as harsh of mouth and as tough of mind as she is easy of virtue. But Defoe's Moll Flanders has, after all, the advantage of early and extended contact with gentility, and it remains her great ambition to be a proper gentlewoman. If circumstances eventually lead her to walk the streets, she still feels that she really should be sitting in respectable homes, and she scrupulously avoids the language, the mannerisms, and the ways of thinking of the gutter. In any case, Moll's outspokenness and her ability to be tough-minded have something peculiar about them; a close consideration of these qualities in the Newgate-born lady of fortune may lead to a more precise understanding of her distinctive attitude toward the world.

Defoe assures us in the preface that his anti-heroine "is made to tell her own tale in modester words than she told it at first." About one thing Moll's account of her career of sin is indeed almost chastely reticent. She usually manages to skirt the physical act by which she makes her way in the world with some stratagem of euphemism or circumlocution. "I by little and little yielded to everything, so that, in a word, he did what he pleased with me; I need say no more."

Her husbands and lovers never lie with her, but "offer her a kindness in that way," "offer something of that kind," or "go to that which they call the last favor." At best, Moll simply fits her illicit unions into a general moral category without designating their particular nature; characteristically, she describes her amours with the older brother of her foster family as "our crime" and "our wicked pleasure." Though this kind of genteel euphemism is a familiar convention in English criminal biographies, there is good reason to suppose that its use in *Moll Flanders* represents an important step toward the realistic employment of language for characterization. A strong sense of reserve

"A Bourgeois Picaroon." From Rogue's Progress: Studies in the Picaresque Novel *by Robert Alter (Cambridge: Harvard University Press, 1964), pp. 35–57. Copyright 1964 by the President and Fellows of Harvard College. Reprinted by permission of the author and the publisher.*

about sexual matters is, as we shall see, entirely consistent with Moll's whole mental make-up.

But what makes this degree of reticence in Moll somewhat surprising is the contrasting brutal frankness of which she is capable. When, for example, the anti-heroine wants to tell us that her incestuous marriage with her American husband is physically disgusting to her, she minces no words. "Everything added to make cohabiting with him the most nauseous thing to me in the world; and I think verily it was come to such a height, that I could almost as willingly have embraced a dog as have let him offer anything of that kind to me, for which reason I could not bear the thoughts of coming between the sheets with him."

Defoe's would-be gentlewoman, in spite of her own frequent resort to euphemism about sexual matters, has a habit of cutting sharply through all camouflaging phraseology and rapping out harsh realities in the short, unambiguous syllables of what she herself calls "plain English." Thus she sums up the career of a thieving couple with which she briefly collaborated: "She was not his wife, but they were partners, it seems, in the trade they carried on, and partners in something else. In short, they robbed together, lay together, were taken together, and at last were hanged together." She treats an insidious proposal from the old governess in the same vigorously candid fashion. "She said something that looked as if she could help me off with my burthen sooner, if I was willing; or, in English, that she could give me something to make me miscarry." Moll is just as quick to give the most unambiguous name to a chief source of the governess' income. " 'Tis scarce credible what practice she had, as well abroad as at home, and yet all upon the private account, or, in plain English, the whoring account."

It is worth noting, moreover, that these moments of unmitigated candor in Moll are by no means limited to her judgments of other people. She is just as ready to put the plainest label of condemnation on her own actions. When, for example, the politic governess tells pregnant Moll, "You must e'en do as other conscientious mothers have done before you," Moll at once makes the appropriate unspoken observation. "I understood what she meant by conscientious mothers; she would have said conscientious whores." Moll's unflinching honesty with herself reveals itself very clearly in an exchange with her first seducer. The wanton young gentleman, after half a year of intimate relations with Moll, has suggested that she marry his brother.

"But here, my dear," says he, ". . . you shall always have my respect, and my sincere affection; . . . you shall be my dear sister, as now you are my dear—" and there he stopped.

"Your dear whore," says I, "you would have said if you had gone on, and you might as well have said; but I understand you."

It is tempting to conclude that all these instances of frankness in Defoe's anti-heroine reflect an admirable—and particularly picaresque —kind of candor. The picaroon in general is an individual who does not act according to "official" morality because, observing how such morality is more frequently preached than practiced, he realizes that he must ignore much of it in order to get along in the world. Since he has no set place in society and is not committed to the established order, he is free from the tribute of lip service to conventional morality which most people feel is exacted from them. He can call a thief a thief and a whore a whore, even when he is the thief or his wife is the whore.

But the case is quite different with Moll Flanders. Her candor, as I shall try to show, derives from a highly unpicaresque source. It is a kind of candor, we might note at the outset, that extends over only one part of her experience. Far more significant than Moll's moments of reticence is a real failure of conscience—certainly from a picaresque viewpoint—in the account she gives of her life. The tough-minded honesty that made her insist on the appellation "whore" when she deserved it all but evaporates after Moll and her Lancastershire husband settle in America with a stock of capital accumulated from prostitution, shoplifting, housebreaking, pickpocketing, and armed robbery on the road. Her perfunctory twinge of conscience over the source of the wealth is quickly overcome by the sense of well-being in finally setting up a comfortable, respectable, and dependably profitable establishment.

The fact is that Moll is not nearly so witheringly honest with herself as some of her moments of frankness might lead one to conclude. Moll's creator, of course, was not only a journalist-novelist but also a steadfast Dissenter, and he may well be speaking sincerely when he asserts in the preface that his book is meant "to discourage and expose all sorts of vice and corruption of manners." This moralist's impulse in Defoe partly explains why his lady of fame is made to call herself bluntly by the name her actions earn her. Moll, a Puritan in all but virtue, generally shies away from words that evoke the physical actuality of her polygamies and prostitutions, but she shows no hesitancy in branding herself a whore because it is a word that is used not so much to describe as to denounce, not to call forth an image but to affirm a stern moral judgment. What, then, has happened to the rigorous moralist when this mistress of many thieving trades arrives at her happy ending, tranquil in mind with the accumulated profits of years of crime?

The disparity between the anti-heroine's vigorous self-condemnation in the main body of the novel and her surprisingly easy conscience at the end of the book offers only an apparent contradiction. It is not really true that Moll is harder on herself as a practitioner of love for profit than as a retired thief. The language is harsher when she speaks of her amorous misdeeds, but her self-condemnation remains a superficial one. And there is a reason for this harshness of language which is quite distinct from the moralist's ends that Defoe may have felt he was realizing.

Moll's propensity for plain-dealing words is in fact directly connected with one peculiar habit of speech that appears with almost annoying frequency in the course of her narration. She repeatedly tacks onto nouns of a certain kind qualifying explanations introduced by phrases like "that is to say," "as I called him," "as it is called." The various characters, for example, who have some kind of dual or false identity in the novel are continually referred to with the addition of such explanatory phrases. When Moll goes on her trip to Lancastershire with the young lady who later proves to be a swindler, Moll, as narrator, cannot conceal her retrospective awareness of the false identity of those involved in the plan to swindle her. "Well, I went with my friend, as I called her, into Lancastershire"; "Her uncle, as she called him, sent a coach and four horses for us." "My friend, who called him brother . . ." An adopted bastard in the house of Moll's accomplice and mentor must be described as "my governess's grandchild, as she called her." Once Moll has discovered that her American husband is also her brother, she does not hesitate to make the forbidden duality of their relationship painfully explicit. "I was now fully resolved to go up point-blank to my brother (husband)."

In general, Moll is uncomfortable using any word whose referent is not altogether clear and unambiguous to her. So she describes a storm on her voyage home from America, "The ship sprung her mainmast, as they called it." Moll, on her part, is not sure exactly what a mainmast is, and she will not take responsibility for the word. This desire for perfect clarity leads her to a suspicion of all figurative language. In the rare instances when she slips into using a metaphor, she is quick to explain its literal meaning or at least to apologize for using it. "This he took for a favor, and so laid down the cudgels, that is to say, the pen." "In the sixty-first year of my age, I launched out into a new world, as I may call it."

The significance of this stylistic habit may become clearer when we recall a memorable figure in English literature before Moll who had a similar mannerism. Shakespeare's Jew of Venice, like Defoe's lady of Newgate, mistrusts the imagination and the language of metaphor that pertains to the imagination. "Water-thieves and land-thieves," he says to Bassanio, and then quickly explains, "I mean pirates." Later he warns Jessica to "stop up my house's ears, I mean my casements." [1]

---

[1] *The Merchant of Venice*, I, iii, 23–24; II, iv, 34.

Moll and Shylock are both outsiders, and in the case of each this habit of speech may reflect, at least in part, the speaker's sense of not belonging to the world of which he speaks. (The picaroon, on the other hand, is an outsider who generally manages to feel at home in his world.) Moreover, Shylock's suspicion of the poetic is as characteristic of his mercantile bent as it is of his outsider's unsureness, and we may infer from the curious parallel between Shylock and Moll that her own attitude toward the imagination and toward the uses of language is very much on the side of the moneylenders.

By contrast, a kind of nimbleness of imagination is a fairly constant component of the picaresque make-up; it is what endows the picaroon with the lightness of heart that wins our affections as well as with the inventiveness that enables him to lighten his neighbor's pockets. Moll Flanders, on the other hand, apart from rare moments of brightness like her first relationship with Jemmy, is anything but lighthearted. A real, red-blooded picaro, in the style of Lazarillo de Tormes or Gil Blas, is a man of imagination by calling. Born in—or rather outside of—a hierarchical society where each individual is assigned a fixed place, he can envisage for himself the possibility of assuming multiple roles. Life is not for him a cut-and-dried product which the buyer must accept exactly as it is handed him, but rather a plastic material which the artistic individual can shape in any of numerous ways. The picaroon has no difficulty in imagining something which can participate in more than one identity at the same time—as witness Lazarillo's angelic tinker and Gil Blas's netherworld highwaymen. His manner of conceiving things is frequently metaphoric because he has a keen awareness of the potential multiplicity of the nature of things.

Moll Flanders, however, insists on living in a world of cold, hard facts. She likes reality to stand still—so that it can be counted—not to shimmer, not to flow from one identity to another, not to comprehend, even for a fleeting moment, a thing and its opposite. The contrast between her kind of mind and that mentality which is characteristically picaresque is reflected in the different attitudes the two take toward disguise. In premodern society, clothing was not only decorative and protective, but had a very definite and important emblematic function. The garment was a clear and fixed symbol of class and calling. The picaroon, in escaping from the fixity of the social system, inevitably becomes a quick-change artist with a large and varied wardrobe. He not only uses disguise adeptly for highly practical purposes, but—as is true for most comic characters—the activity of disguise is something in which he delights. In slipping off one costume and putting on another, he affirms his protean nature, he achieves a sense of the broad range of possibilities of what he, the picaroon, can be.

Moll Flanders, on the other hand, remains wholly Moll Flanders

even when the exigencies of her career in thieving lead her to go out
in disguise. Putting on different clothes does not mean for her putting
on a new identity, or even playing a new role. She is in fact as uncomfortable with the idea that Moll Flanders can be anyone else, as she is
with the idea that an adopted girl can be the governess' "grandchild,"
or that Jemmy's fellow conspirator is his "sister." It is instructive to
note that the two disguises in which Moll feels most uneasy—almost
guilty—are a man's clothes and a beggar's rags. Of the various costumes
she puts on, these are the two which most contradict her own fixed
nature; the one denies her sex, the other her constant need to preserve
personal propriety. In the latter case, she is literally punished for
descending so far from herself: she gets no profit from it, and she
resolves never to resort to such a low disguise again. Interestingly,
Shylock, Moll's literal-minded mercantile predecessor, is as much at
a loss as she in the face of exchanged identities; he is finally undone
by a woman playing a man's role with consummate skill.

Defoe's quasi-picaresque heroine is, in the last analysis, a very serious
businesswoman. She cannot cope with a complex, multiple, contradictory reality; she must break it down into counters that have clear
and unequivocal values stamped on their faces. She calls a whore a
whore not so much out of moral honesty as out of moral literal-mindedness. She will not let people ease an act out of the straightforward,
unambiguous category in which she has been taught it belongs: you
either are or you aren't, and—rather than suffer the faintest uneasiness
of doubt—Moll is quick to say that she is.

This anti-heroine's tough-mindedness, in sum, is largely a result of
her literal-mindedness. At several points in the narrative, her handling
of language clearly suggests the close connection between these two
qualities. Early in the novel, when the younger brother of Moll's foster
family becomes enamored of her, the mother begins to show some
animosity toward the parish child that she has taken into her home.
"In short, his mother had let fall some speeches, as if she intended
to put me out of family; that is, in English, to turn me out of doors."
Moll tears away the veil of euphemism because she wants to name the
thing plainly and exactly by its right name, and a necessary concomi-
tant to her verbal literalism is a moral literalism. She insists on the
blunt phrase for what Robin's mother wants to do, and consequently
she faces the unadorned harshness of the mother's intentions toward
her. . . .

E. A. Baker, in his *History of the English Novel*, has recognized
that *Moll Flanders* is a picaresque novel only in its surface qualities,
though it seems to me that he offers a rather misleading idea of what
kind of book it really is. "Except in its autobiographical procedure,
incidents succeeding each other with the chance disconnexion of real

life, there is nothing of the picaresque in *Moll Flanders*. The heroine is a rogue, but not one rejoicing in her rogueries. To the modern reader, her life is a serious study of the effects of heredity and environment in the making of criminals."[2]

The last suggestion can be dismissed as a somewhat unfortunate lapse in historical perspective. There is no point in trying to make Defoe into a kind of eighteenth-century Zola. If he has some rudimentary notions of social and hereditary causes for crime, they are considerably more primitive than the modern conceptions first fully articulated in the nineteenth century, and they are certainly not the central concern of his novels.

What is more instructive in Baker's comment is his observation that Moll is no picaroon because she is a rogue who does not rejoice in her rogueries. The picaro engages in a variety of cheating practices in order to obtain money, but it is never solely in order to obtain money. It would be an exaggeration to say that the picaroon is indifferent to money: he views it as the wherewithal he must have to satisfy his needs and desires, and therefore the more of it he can get, the better off he is. But money does not become for him the single consuming end to which all means are subservient. The picaroon does delight in his rogueries for their own sake. They are for him not only a means of making profit, but a magnificent game affording an opportunity for the exercise of art and ingenuity. If we were to associate his profiteering activities with any kind of capitalism, it would have to be the "adventurer's capitalism" that [Max] Weber identifies with the economically traditionalist[3] society. The picaroon's methods of enriching himself are, in Weber's terms, clearly not "rational"; it is the continual newness of adventure in his various profitable pursuits which attracts him.

In point of historical fact, this very spirit of economic adventurism played a rather important part in the growth of modern British capitalism, as Charles and Katherine George have recently pointed out in their closely documented study *The Protestant Mind of the English Reformation*.[4] Defoe's protagonist in this case turns out to be more Weberian than the complex historical phenomenon Weber was analyzing. For there is decidedly little spirit of adventure in the rogueries of Moll Flanders. Her variety of extralegal activities is not in the least

[2] E. A. Baker, *The History of the English Novel*, 9 vols. (London: H. F. and G. Witherly, 1929), III, 190.

[3] For Weber's explanation of the traditionalist society as distinguished from modern capitalist society, see his *The Protestant Ethic and the Spirit of Capitalism*, trans. Talcott Parsons (New York: Charles Scribner's Sons, 1958), pp. 58f.

[4] Charles H. and Katherine George, *The Protestant Mind of the English Reformation: 1570–1640*. (Princeton: Princeton University Press, 1961), p. 147.

a game for her; on the contrary, she envisages virtually everything she does as a very serious business. The act of love itself is no more than a piece of stock-in-trade for the hard-working Puritan Moll; she certainly never gives the faintest hint of any pleasure or emotional involvement in connection with it. She views nearly all her activities as means of making profit. One could hardly find a clearer antithesis to the picaresque attitude toward money, its significance, and its uses. In this respect, Moll is the most duty-bound of Defoe's protagonists. Crusoe at least takes a more perceptible measure of delight and satisfaction in the management of his assorted home industries, and there are some occasional glimmerings of a spirit of adventure or spontaneity in Colonel Jack, Captain Singleton, and Roxana. But weighed against the model of picaresque buoyancy, all the central figures of Defoe's fictions have a leaden seriousness, and they move in a different sphere of imaginative existence from that of the continental picaro.

From the very outset of her career, money exercises an uncontrollable fascination over Moll Flanders. In exchange for the first furtive caresses allowed to the older brother of her foster family, she is given money, and it is the money which immediately grips her imagination. "I was more confounded with the money than I was before with the love, and began to be so elevated that I scarce knew the ground I stood on." And she can hardly withdraw her attention from this mesmerizing acquisition. "As for the gold, I spent whole hours in looking upon it; I told the guineas over a thousand times a day." When Moll finally takes her first lover it is the proposal of a hundred guineas a year together with a first payment in advance which overwhelms her. "My colour came and went, at the sight of the purse and with the fire of his proposal together, so that I could not say a word, and he easily perceived it; so putting the purse into my bosom, I made no more resistance to him, but let him do just what he pleased, and as often as he pleased."

From this point on, Moll makes it very clear to her readers that her principal motive in whatever she does is profit. She measures people and their relationship to her almost solely by the consideration of how much money can be got out of them. "As for me, my business was his money, and what I could make of him." "I had no spleen at the saucy rogue, nor were his admissions anything to me, since there was nothing to be got by him." Moll does not even take credit for a temporary period of celibacy, but freely admits that the lack of opportunity for profit was the only reason for her virtue, as the attraction of remuneration was all that could tempt that virtue. "I was not wicked enough to come into the crime for the mere vice of it, and I had no extraordinary offers that tempted me with the main thing which I wanted."

Whatever the dubious bypaths on which Moll sets her shapely feet, she always keeps her eye fixed firmly on the pound sterling. She is able to let the idea of profit override all moral considerations with such facility that one may well wonder if the conscience of Defoe the moralist has not been carried away by the imagination of Defoe the lifelong entrepreneur. He has his protagonist report one illicit venture in as glib a manner as this: "He stopped the coach at a house where, it seems, he was acquainted, and where they made no scruple to show us upstairs into a room with a bed in it. At first I seemed to be unwilling to go up, but after a few words I yielded to that too, being willing to see the end of it, and in hopes to make something of it at last. As for the bed, etc., I was not much concerned about that part."

Whether it is a question of robbing a drunken gentleman with whom she has gone to bed or contracting a legitimate marriage with a man who is the soul of probity, Moll's attitude is the same. The banker who helps her with her finances treats her with the greatest decency and frankness in every respect, but she sees him wholly in terms of how much profit he will bring. "I played with this lover as an angler with a trout . . . I made no scruple in my thoughts of quitting my honest citizen, whom I was not so much in love with as not to leave him for a richer."

The moral universe of *Moll Flanders*, we find, is bare and depressingly cold. If the accumulation of money is the only important goal in human life, such things as love, friendship, the pleasures of the body and the mind, become highly suspect distractions, and one is forced to mistrust all other human beings as competitors and possible depredators. Ian Watt offers an interesting suggestion that the very flatness and sketchiness of psychology in the characters that surround Moll Flanders may reflect not a failure of imagination but an attempt at faithful representation of the effects on personal relationships of the criminal milieu. Watt probably gives too much credit to Defoe's art, but his sense of what has happened to human relations in Defoe's world is sound. We may add that the criminal milieu of the novel is in some important respects simply the capitalist milieu writ large, even if Defoe was not altogether conscious of the parallel. "Moll Flanders, and most of Defoe's other characters," Watt writes, "all belong on Crusoe's island; especially solitary, they take a severely functional view of their fellows." [5]

One need not suppose, of course, that every capitalist lived in constant dread of betrayal by all whom he encountered. The whole idea of credit, so essential to the capitalist system, is based on the probity of the individual entrepreneur, that is, ultimately, on mutual trust. But relentless economic competition also quite naturally could make

[5] Ian Watt, *The Rise of the Novel* (Berkeley and Los Angeles: University of California Press, 1957), p. 112.

men wary of one another, and here again Moll's career represents the
full realization of a possibility distinctly inherent in the capitalist
situation. Her suspicion toward her fellow men is nearly relentless.
There are only two people in her life to whom she becomes perceptibly
attached, and even to them she only partly opens herself. The relationship between Moll and her governess is initiated entirely out of util-
itarian motives, though a strong mutual loyalty develops afterward
between the two women. The loyalty is strong, at least, on the part
of the governess, who goes to great pains to help Moll where she badly
needs help. The younger woman professes to her readers an equal feeling of affection for the governess, but she is solely a beneficiary in the
relationship and does nothing on her part to prove her affection.
Genuine devotion to another person would scarcely have been credible in Moll, and, in keeping with her general character, she is careful
to conceal from the old lady much of her private life and past.

The same is true in the anti-heroine's relationship with her Lancastershire husband. The mutual revelation of the two would-be deceivers
—the scene which E. M. Forster admires so much[6]—is a moment of
real picaresque camaraderie; but when the lovers soon after take leave
of one another, Moll makes certain to indicate that "still I reserved
the grand secret, and never broke my resolution, which was not to let
him ever know my true name, who I was, or where to be found." Even
when the two come to America together as man and wife, she does not
let him in on the zealously guarded secret of how much money she
really has.

In contrast to this ethos of suspicion which relates to the predatory
aspects of modern capitalism, the picaresque capacity for openness and
companionship retains connections with an older social and economic
system. One of the principal traits which distinguished traditionalist
societies from their capitalist successors was the strong sense of community that pervaded the older kind of social organization.[7] A man
did not regard himself wholly as an individual in the modern sense,
that is, a distinct, separate, independent entity. He saw himself as
part of a social organism. One can hardly suppose that there was no
element of competitive struggle in the medieval local community, but
more important was a deeply rooted feeling of mutual responsibility
among the members of the community.[8]

[6] E. M. Forster, *Aspects of the Novel* (New York: Harcourt, Brace, and Co., 1927),
pp. 91–92.
[7] For a concise and lucid discussion of the precapitalist sense of community, see
L. C. Knights, *Drama and Society in the Age of Jonson* (London: Chatto and
Windus, 1936), pp. 17f.
[8] Many rural areas of the American South, at least until fairly recently, embodied
one particular variety of this precapitalist sense of community. Faulkner's novel *The*

When the picaresque novel first makes its appearance in sixteenth-century Spain, the cohesiveness of community of the medieval world is already in the process of disintegrating. The picaro determines to fend for himself partly because he is an individual who would not fit into the communal pattern in any case, but also because the weave of the pattern itself has begun to pull apart. Even so, he still preserves something of the traditionalist sense of mutual responsibility, the kind of responsibility developed in an organic community not only among individuals, but between trade or calling and the people it serves, and between one class and another. We have only to recall Lazarillo's disinterested loyalty to the indigent squire, or Gil Blas's virtually feudal devotion to Don Alphonse and his family.

Defoe's anti-heroine, on the other hand, has no real sense of responsibility toward other human beings or even toward herself, that is, toward the fulfillment of her own desires or the development of her own potentialities as a person. The only responsibility she does feel—and it is quite literally a responsibility for her—is toward the accumulation of wealth for its own sake. Weber's description of the practical philosophy of Benjamin Franklin could easily serve as a portrait of Moll and an explanation of her activities.

> The peculiarity of the philosophy of avarice appears to be . . . above all the idea of a duty of the individual toward the increase of his capital, which is assumed as an end in itself.[9]
>
> In fact, the *summum bonum* of this ethic, the earning of more and more money, combined with the strict avoidance of all spontaneous enjoyment of life, is above all completely devoid of any eudaemonistic, not to say hedonistic, admixture. It is thought of so purely as an end in itself that from the point of view of the happiness of, or utility to, the single individual, it appears entirely transcendental and absolutely irrational.[10]

Again, one may question whether such "worldly asceticism" was in fact the dominant spirit in the rise of capitalism, but Moll's long career as a thief is certainly characterized by precisely this kind of single-minded duty to the increase of capital. On rational grounds, it is not easy to explain her persistence in crime once she has amassed enough money to support herself comfortably for the rest of her days.

Hamlet presents a vivid picture of a capitalist ethic encroaching upon Southern traditionalism. Flem Snopes, with all his hard-eyed, fast-dealing kinsmen, moves in on the sleepy townlet of Frenchman's Bend. The old sense of social and economic community, most strikingly represented by V. K. Ratliff, easy-going itinerant sewing machine salesman and cousin to everyone, yields to the aggressive enterprise of the Snopeses, a clan in which the closest blood cousins would not dare trust one another.

[9] Weber, *Protestant Ethic*, p. 51.

[10] Ibid., p. 53.

After all, Moll gets no pleasure from the act of theft itself, except for a mild feeling of satisfaction at having achieved a special competence in a trade. The anti-heroine as a matter of fact is constantly terrified in her criminal activities over the risks involved; the thrill of danger has no appeal for her because she is a good bourgeoise who wants both security and an assured profit in her enterprises.[11] And she certainly does not increase her spending with the increase of her stock of money. Throughout her changes in fortune, she maintains the same standard of living: simple, never ostentatious, but always proper.

Moll's persistence in her career of crime offers an exact parallel to the familiar case of the businessman who cannot bring himself to retire from his business, even when he has made more money than he can use, because profit-making has become for him the only meaningful activity in life. And the various aspects of the thief's calling as described in *Moll Flanders* are consistently analogous to the daily business of a legitimate entrepreneur. Defoe's shoplifter and pickpocket repeatedly refers to her particular manner of acquiring wealth as "the trade." Like any trade, it must be managed with skill and, above all, with prudence. Like most lines of business, it has its on-seasons and off-seasons. "But the city was thin, and I thought our trade felt it a little, as well as other." After Moll's venture to Harwich, she learns that her business, like many others, is best carried out on a safe domestic basis without undue risks in a foreign market. "I was now returned to London, and though by the accident of the last adventure I got something considerable, yet I was not fond of any more country rambles, nor should I have ventured abroad again if I had carried the trade on to the end of my days."

A sound instinct led Defoe, merchant and entrepreneur, to present thievery in terms of capitalist enterprise. We can go beyond the writer's own intention to observe that the effect of his representing the thief in this light is to expose some of the most essential—and most unattractive—traits of the capitalist. (John Gay, in fact, just six years after the appearance of *Moll Flanders,* was to make conscious satirical use of such a parallel between the respectable world and the underworld in *The Beggar's Opera.*) The acquisition of wealth, when the individual has no real responsibility to anything beyond acquisition itself, can quickly become an activity of pure depredation: the equation of capitalist and thief is not entirely an inappropriate one. Moll Flanders can have such an amazingly easy conscience about her crimes because, however much she professes the contrary, they are not really crimes for

[11] This is why Moll, after one successful attempt at the gaming table (frequently a favorite place for picaresque diversion), vows never to gamble again. She does not object to robbery since it is a surer kind of venture, but gambling must be avoided as a deadly sin because it involves a very high risk of good capital.

her. The only act that she could sense profoundly as criminal would be for her to shirk her duty to accumulate capital. We can listen to Moll playing lip service to the traditional morality she claims to accept, but she goes on immediately to the matters of finance which are her real concern. "We had £354 between us, but a worse gotten estate was scarce ever put together to begin the world with. Our greatest misfortune as to our stock was that it was all in money, which every one knows is an unprofitable cargo to be carried to the plantations." And nothing could illustrate more clearly how little guilt Moll really feels over her thefts than the moment when she makes a present of a watch stolen at a prayer meeting to her dear, rediscovered American son. Moll tenderly asks him to kiss the watch now and then for her sake, while she calmly observes, "I did not indeed tell him that I had stole it from a gentlewoman's side, at a meeting-house in London. That's by the way."

Defoe's anti-heroine is made frequently to express her dismay over her life of sin and her apprehension of the divine judgment to which she must be called. There is little ground to doubt the honesty of Defoe's pious intentions, but it is clear also that his imaginative grasp of hell and damnation goes no further than the walls of Newgate prison. To be within these walls, amid "the hellish noise, the roaring, swearing, and clamour, the stench and nastiness, and all the dreadful afflicting things," is the most abject and pitiful state in which Defoe can imagine a human soul to be plunged. This is where the bankrupt—the damned of individualistic capitalism[12]—are sent to suffer for their mortal sin of insolvency. This is where thieves who have had the indiscretion to be caught—the underworld equivalent to bankruptcy among capitalists—are held till their final judgment is carried out. And this is where Defoe himself was committed for five dark months which he would never be able to forget. Nothing could be more hateful to the sturdy burgher than the complete descent from propriety that prison life forces on him: the bad odors and foul language, the dirt, the rags, the vermin. And nothing could be more maddening for the hardy entrepreneur than to be cut off by imprisonment from the possibility of regular profit-making.

It is not surprising that, since the hell of *Moll Flanders* lies no deeper than the foundation stones of Newgate, there is one universally efficacious golden bough with which a soul can descend into "all the horrors of that dismal place," and return unscathed. For the literalist Defoe, of course, the golden bough is literally gold and nothing else.

[12] Balzac's *César Birotteau* makes painfully clear what a dismal fate bankruptcy is for the entrepreneur. As Birotteau's grandeur and decline indicate, the social disgrace of bankruptcy is in itself an agonizing "punishment" for that deadly sin, even without a prison sentence.

As long as a man possesses an adequate supply of cash, he need fear no evil. "I knew that with money in the pocket, one is at home everywhere." (We might note the sharp contrast between this capitalist's aphorism and the picaresque attitude: the picaroon is at home everywhere with a portion of native wit in his head.) When Moll goes out shoplifting, she is in the habit of taking with her a substantial amount of coin of the realm as a kind of protective charm. Once, when she is nearly caught, the alderman who is called in to question her declares her absolute innocence as soon as he perceives the magic sign of gold in her pocket. The ultimate assurance that Moll's governess can give her in the despair of her imprisonment is to remind her, "Why, you have money, have you not?" And once Moll is put on board ship as a convicted felon, the sight of her swollen purse immediately dazzles the crewmen and officers and transforms her state from prisoner for transportation to emigrating lady of quality.

This all-importance of money does not, however, make the concerns of Defoe's novel in any way petty. As Virginia Woolf has observed, quite the contrary is true. Because money—or the possibility of making money—is ultimately equated by Defoe's protagonists with life itself, it becomes for them something enormous, challenging, mysterious, perilous.[13]

One could find no better summary for the kind of significance money possesses in the world of *Moll Flanders* than these words of admonition which appear in a seventeenth-century capitalist tract entitled *The Worth of a Peny or a Caution to Keep Money*. "Whosoever wanteth money is ever subject to contempt and scorne in the world, let him be furnished with never so good gifts, either of body or mind . . . In these times we may say with the wise man: . . . better it is to die than be poore, for now money is the worlds God . . . it gives birth, beauty, honour, and credit . . . *Pecuniae omnia obediunt:* hence it is so admired that millions venture both soules and bodies for the possession of it.[14]

If the characters in Defoe's novels never admit so frankly that money is their god, money is certainly the one sure sign for them that grace has been granted them by the God of the Christians. Here, of course, it is appropriate to recall Weber's discussion of the Puritan understanding of worldly success and its positive spiritual implications.[15] Moll Flanders is overwhelmed with gratefulness to Providence when

---

[13] Virginia Woolf, *The Common Reader* (London: Hogarth Press, 1929), pp. 130–131. [Virginia Woolf's comments on Defoe are reprinted on pp. 11–16 of this volume.]

[14] Henry Peacham, *The Worth of a Peny or a Caution to Keep Money* (London: privately printed, 1647), p. 15.

[15] See Weber, *Protestant Ethic*, pp. 162f.

her son surprises her with the news of a £100 a year income for her. Afterward, when Moll puts down the £100 in silver before her husband, together with a purse full of pistoles, he goes into the raptures of a prayer-meeting epiphany. "Says my husband, 'So is Heaven's goodness sure to work the same effects in all sensible minds, where mercies touch the heart!' lifted up both hands, and with an ecstasy of joy, 'What is God a-doing,' says he, 'for such an ungrateful dog as I am!' "

And it is true, at least in one sense, that *Moll Flanders* is a fundamentally religious novel. If we adopt the broad definition of religion suggested by the modern existentialist theologians—an activity directed toward an ultimate concern—Moll can be described as a believer never remiss in her religious duties. In this respect, Defoe's novel looks not at all backward to the picaresque tradition, but forward to the nineteenth century, to Balzac and the portrayal in the novel of the all-consuming quest for wealth. Moll's literary cousins are not Guzman and Gil Blas, but Félix Grandet and Mr. Dombey. It is one of the essential characteristics of the picaroon's nature not to get involved in religious causes, whether the inner sanctum of the religion is in the Vatican or at the Bourse. The picaroon really has no ultimate concerns. He lives from day to day, seeking the means to fulfill his natural needs and desires from day to day. He does not clench his will into a single-purposed effort that comprehends every part of his life. There is a perceptible relaxation of existential seriousness in the picaresque novels: here, one feels, is life as it could be lived, with difficulties to overcome, but without crushing responsibilities to bear. In the world of *Moll Flanders,* however, the individual must carry the weight of a single unending responsibility which necessarily converts the conduct of his life into an austere discipline.

It would seem, then, more misleading than instructive to call *Moll Flanders* a picaresque novel. It has one general, coincidental similarity with the picaresque narratives—it is the episodic fictional autobiography of a "roguish" figure—but it derives from the English criminal biography, not from the line of *Lazarillo;* and its sense of life, its imaginative atmosphere, and its moral feeling are in most significant respects antithetical to those of the picaresque novel. The profound difference between Moll's single-minded discipline and the distinctively picaresque mode of existence becomes strikingly clear when a quarter of a century after the publication of Defoe's novel, the continental picaro makes a full-dress appearance on English soil in the person of Roderick Random.

Moll Flanders

by George A. Starr

Our human sympathies must sometimes be at odds with our moral judgments: this principle resonates through the writings of Defoe. In the *Review*, he points out that "the Scripture bids us not despise . . . a Thief, who steals to satisfie his Hunger; not that the Man is less a Thief, but despise him not, you that know not what Hunger is." [1] In another gloss on Proverbs 6:30 two decades later, Defoe says, "the very Text itself speaks, tho' not in favour of the Crime, yet in great Compassion and Pity for the Criminal Men." [2] Robinson Crusoe develops the same argument: I do not pretend, he says, "that these circumstances render my failing, or any man's else, the less a sin, but they make the reason why we that have fallen should rather be pitied than reproached by those who think they stand, because, when the same assaults are made upon the chastity of their honour, it may be every jot as likely to be prostituted as their neighbour's." [3] In the same vein, Roxana stresses the role of poverty in inducing her to become her landlord's mistress, but is careful to add, "not that I plead this as a Justification of my Conduct, but that it may move the Pity, even of those that abhor the Crime." [4] Throughout *Moll Flanders* it is assumed that the respectable reader abhors crime and despises thieves, and that (as one critic has said of Moll herself) he "struggles with no confusion as to

---

"Moll Flanders." *From* Defoe and Casuistry *by George A. Starr (To be published and copyright 1971 by Princeton University Press). Reprinted by permission of Princeton University Press.*

[1] *Review*, facsimile ed. Arthur W. Secord, 22 vols. (New York, 1938), V (February 8, 1709), 543–44; cf. *Serious Reflections*, in *Romances and Narratives of Daniel Defoe*, ed. George A. Aitken, 16 vols. (1895), III, 35.

[2] *The Compleat English Tradesman*, 2 vols. (1727), II, 293; cf. also *The Just Complaint of the Poor Weavers* (1719), p. 5.

[3] *Serious Reflections*, in *Romances and Narratives*, III, 55.

[4] *Roxana*, ed. Jane Jack (1964), p. 39; cf. *Mercurius Politicus* for January 1717, in which Defoe, personating a Whig who has contributed to the relief of Jacobite prisoners in Lancaster Castle, is told by a friend, "*but they are our Enemies*, and I am sure you abhor them." "So I do," he replies, "I abhor their crime, but I pity their persons" (in William Lee, *Daniel Defoe: His Life and Recently Discovered Writings*, 3 vols. [1869], II, 4).

what is right and what is wrong," but accepts "a classical moralism which drew a sharp line between goodness and badness." [5] Much of the book seeks to support this "classical moralism," not to subvert it: from the preface onwards, we are invited to abhor Moll's crimes, but urged not to despise the criminal herself. We are asked to distinguish between act and agent—between what Moll does and what she essentially is: without minimizing her culpability, the narrative seeks to deflect our severity from the doer to the deed, and to retain sympathy for the erring heroine.

This kind of appeal to the reader is most overt when she is about to commit her first theft, and plays an important part elsewhere in the book as well. But it is not the only pattern in which sympathy and judgment are related. At times, Moll's story tends to subvert "classical moralism," and casts doubt on the legitimacy of rigid distinctions between "goodness and badness." With this object, considerable emphasis is put on the principle that circumstances alter cases. William Perkins, the Puritan father of English casuistry, had asserted a century earlier that "the circumstances of time, place, person, and manner of doing, doe serve to enlarge or extenuate the sin committed," [6] and Defoe frequently reiterates this concept. "Few things in nature are simply unlawful and dishonest," he observes in one work, "but . . . all crime is made so by the addition and concurrence of circumstances"; "Circumstances, Time, and Place alter things very much," he says in another; elsewhere, that "as Sin is Circumstantiated, those Accounts are sinful under one Government, which are not so under another"; and that "what may be simply Lawful, may be unlawful *Circumstantially*." [7] Moll never explicitly maintains that her extraordinary situation alters the sinful or criminal character of an action, but she often adduces circumstances that servé to palliate if not justify what she has just done or is about to do. In the process, the notion that an act is inherently right or wrong is at least called in question; moral judgment, it is suggested, must take into account the total context of a given act, and the context often works to Moll's advantage.

These are two of the ways, then, in which Moll seems to me to gain

[5] Carl Van Doren, Introduction to *Moll Flanders* (New York, 1923), pp. xii, xiii. All citations of *Moll Flanders* in the text refer to the World's Classics edition, ed. Herbert Davis, with an Introduction by Bonamy Dobrée (1961)—the only modern reprint based on the first edition.

[6] *The Whole Treatise of the Cases of Conscience* [1606], in *Workes*, 3 vols. (1616–18), II, 11–12.

[7] *The Compleat English Tradesman*, I, 241; cf. I, 97–98, "there are very few things in the world that are simply evil, but things are made circumstantially evil when they are not so in themselves"; *Little Review* (July 4, 1705), pp. 35, 36; *A Letter to Mr. How* [1701], in *A True Collection of the Writings of the Author of the True Born English-man* (1703), p. 336.

and hold our sympathy: she distinguishes her essential self from her admittedly reprehensible doings, but also manages at times to lessen the stigma ordinarily attached to specific acts. Other qualities contribute to the same effect, of course. Moll's independence and vitality are captivating;[8] the candor, the directness, and the very persistence of her speaking voice are disarming;[9] and her siding penitently with the reader against the wayward creature whose former misdeeds she must recount can also be insinuating. I mention various ways in which Moll gains sympathy, partly to make clear that casuistry is not being proposed as the sole means by which she retains our affection, and partly to indicate my grounds for not regarding the book as consistently ironic. Those who find the heroine an object of continual irony imply that we are always coolly judging her and never emotionally involved in what she says or does. My objection to this is not that we never judge her, but that we are not allowed to do so with any such rigor, or from any such comfortable distance, as we might ordinarily adopt in the face of "all the progression of crime which she ran through in three-score years." [10] Sympathy keeps breaking in, and our ironic detachment—along with Defoe's—is tempered by imaginative identification.

The first important episode in Moll's story is her seduction by the elder brother in the Colchester family, which she does not, at the time, regard as a case of conscience at all. On the contrary, she admits that "I gave myself up to a readiness of being ruined without the least concern" (p. 30). So far is she from weighing her situation morally that she does not even think practically; the brother is more deliberate, but Moll reflects that "he made more circumlocution than, if he had known my thoughts, he had occasion for" (p. 31). Her opinion of the preliminaries to her seduction, that "Nothing was ever so stupid on both sides" (p. 30), is thus borne out by the narrative itself. When she says that "I had not one thought of my safety or of my virtue about me" (p. 26), her point is not that she forfeits both, but that she does

---

[8] See especially Ian Watt, *The Rise of the Novel* (1957), p. 132 and passim. A number of Robert Langbaum's remarks about Browning and Tennyson are highly relevant to this aspect of *Moll Flanders*: see "The Dramatic Monologue: Sympathy versus Judgment," in *The Poetry of Experience* (New York, 1963), pp. 75–108.

[9] On these points, see Sheldon Sacks, *Fiction and the Shape of Belief* (Berkeley and Los Angeles, 1964), pp. 267–70, and Martin Price's remark, apropos of a typical scene in *Moll Flanders*, that "Fielding was to make something beautifully ironic of this kind of mixture of motives. Defoe uses it differently; *candor disarms the moral judgment that irony would require* (*To the Palace of Wisdom: Studies in Order and Energy from Dryden to Blake* [Garden City, 1964], p. 276; italics mine).

[10] Preface, pp. 3–4. The debate over irony is surveyed admirably by Ian Watt in "The Recent Critical Fortunes of *Moll Flanders,*" *Eighteenth-Century Studies,* I (1967), 109–26.

so without a thought. By laying so much stress on the folly that precedes the act, and by blaming herself for this folly, she seeks to deflect the reader's judgment from a question of fornication to one of stupidity, and to soften his verdict by emphatically forestalling it herself. The preface claims that this episode has "many happy turns given it to expose the crime, and . . . the foolish, thoughtless, and abhorred conduct of both the parties" (p. 5). Without denying that Moll's behavior is criminal and abhorrent, Defoe emphasizes that it is foolish and thoughtless, and thus enables her to retain sympathy that she would forfeit if her action had been more calculated.

With the same object, all initiative is ascribed to the man, and much is made of Moll's passivity. As she will do on later occasions, she represents herself as carried along by her circumstances (here, the precarious dependence of her role in the Colchester family); by external inducements well adapted to her situation (here, a great deal of gold); and by the persuasiveness and cunning of others (here, a man full of flattery and stratagems, who knows "as well how to catch a woman in his net as a partridge when he went a-setting"). Moll's naiveté is also insisted upon. "Knowing nothing of the wickedness of the times," she is told an "abundance of . . . fine things, which [she], poor fool, did not understand the drift of"; and she acts "as if there was no such things as any kind of love but that which tended to matrimony" (pp. 28–29). The effect of these touches of the *ingénue* is to minimize further the element of deliberate choice on her part, so that she seems to undergo mischief—to be deluded by the promises and entrapped by the wiles of her seducer—rather than to do mischief. Like Eve, Defoe's heroine faces a determined and resourceful adversary, whom she seems ill-equipped to resist.

Along with her passivity and her naiveté, Moll acknowledges her frailty; yet what appear to be confessions may have the effect of raising her, not lowering her, in our esteem. The episode is punctuated by frequent admissions of vanity. But by mentioning that she had mastered French, the harpsichord, singing, dancing, and other genteel skills, and that she was "taken for very handsome, or, if you please, for a great beauty" (p. 22), Moll indicates that her pride was neither groundless nor self-generated. Other confessions of frailty have a similar effect. She admits at one point that "I had no room, as well as no power to have denied him"; and at the moment of her seduction, that "I could not say a word" (pp. 29, 33). She thus suggests that she was overwhelmed, not induced through inclination or interest to give her assent, and by presenting herself in this light—as frail rather than wanton—she further allays our severity. The foregoing details enforce a distinction between an act and its circumstances; in this case, between a seduction and various factors that complicate its moral status.

These complicating factors tend in some degree to displace the actual deed as the object of our attention. Moreover, Moll herself is characterized less by what she does than by an array of motives and pressures that contribute to her seduction. A summary of her overt actions can only lead to the conclusion reached in the preface that they are criminal and abhorrent. Yet what Defoe gives us is anything but a summary of overt actions, and the transfer of emphasis is crucial to our sympathy for the heroine.

After her seduction, Moll's situation is entangled further by the younger brother, who "proposes fairly and honourably" to marry her. "I resisted the proposal with obstinacy," she reports, "I laid before him the inequality of the match; the treatment I should meet with in the family; the ingratitude it would be to his good father and mother, who had taken me into their house upon such generous principles" (pp. 34–35). We might suppose that Moll's conscience is aroused, and that she had begun to weigh her conduct in the light of moral principles, but it is clear that no such awakening has taken place. "I said everything to dissuade him from his design that I could imagine," Moll confesses, "except telling him the truth . . . but that I durst not think of mentioning . . . I repented heartily my easiness with the eldest brother; not from any reflection of conscience, but from a view of the happiness I might have enjoyed, and had now made impossible; for though I had no great scruples of conscience . . . to struggle with, yet I could not think of being a whore to one brother and a wife to the other" (pp. 35, 36). Moll's celebration of legitimate ideals serves to cloak the truth, her repentance of past "easiness" springs from a sense of lost opportunity, and her misgivings over the proposed marriage arise from squeamishness about what she evidently regards as incest. Her reticence towards the younger brother, however, natural and blameless in itself,[11] leads not only to disguise and concealment,

---

[11] Cf. Moll's later remark that "I was not obliged to tell him that I was his brother's whore, though I had no other way to put him off" (p. 67). Jeremy Taylor had observed that *"Nemo tenetur infamare se,* is a rule universally admitted among the casuists, 'no man is bound to discover his own shame'" (*Ductor Dubitantium,* ed. Alexander Taylor, in *Whole Works,* ed. Reginald Heber, rev. Charles P. Eden, 10 vols. [1850], X, 113.) For a case resembling Moll's, and further discussion of the obligation of self-accusation, see the *Athenian Mercury,* IX, No. xxviii, Quest. 2. A young lady confesses that *"A certain lewd and infamous riffler of my Honour . . . has . . . been a little too busie where he had nothing to do: But I'd since the Good Fortune to enter Matrimony with a Person as far above me in Estate as Desert, and . . . manag'd all things so that he knew nothing of the Matter—However, I'm since that extreamly troubled for the Cheat I've put upon him, and the Injury I conceive I have done him . . . Your Advice pray in this Condition?"* The Athenian Society replies, "We'll first give you the Opinion of a late Author, and then our own . . . He tells your Ladyship, 'Your Sin when committed was against Heaven, not your *Honourable Lover* . . . when he made his *Addresses,* you were not oblig'd to be

but to a kind of sophistry which exempts itself from the very sanctions it invokes.

What Moll undergoes, then, is not a crisis of conscience. When she says, "I was now in a very great strait, and really knew not what to do" (p. 37), her perplexity is essentially tactical, not ethical. She produces moral arguments for strategic reasons, not because she regards them as relevant to her own decisions, and as we shall find her doing on various other occasions, she endorses doctrines which she does not feel herself bound by. It is easy enough to deplore her pharisaism and to condemn her failure to take personally the norms of conduct she so persuasively advocates. Nevertheless she herself has acknowledged the existence of moral sanctions, and their hypothetical (if not practical) bearing on her behavior. The resulting impression is not one of hypocrisy—it is from her own mouth, after all, that we learn how far short of her lofty protestations her actions fall—but of disarming candor. However deceptive and evasive she may be towards the younger brother, she seems engagingly open and confidential towards *us*.

When Moll seeks her lover's advice about escaping the other brother's importunate suit, her anxieties are still prudential rather than moral, but they are cast in the form of a traditional case of conscience. The man counsels her to delay giving his brother a firm answer: Moll is startled, and tells him "he knew very well that I had no consent to give; that he had engaged himself to marry me, and that my consent was at the same time engaged to him; that he had all along told me I was his wife, and I looked upon myself as effectually so as if the ceremony had passed" (p. 41). And soon afterwards she declares to him that "I was your wife intentionally, though not in the eyes of the world . . . it was as effectual a marriage . . . as if we had been publicly wedded by the parson of the parish" (pp. 45–46). Two long-debated problems underlie Moll's reproaches to her seducer: what constitutes a valid marriage, and more specifically, what formal ceremony (if any) is required? Moll echoes attitudes that Defoe had expressed two decades earlier, in the "Advice from the Scandal Club," which in turn are based largely on seventeenth-century casuistical

---

your own *Accuser*, and . . . 'twas afterwards no part of yours to unveil the mistake'; and in all this still he is *right*, but here lyes the *Juggel*, Why did you *marry* him, which you ought not in strict *Virtue* and *Honour* to have done . . . You ought to have been the *Wife* of your first Acquaintance, or else always to have liv'd *un-marry'd*, and are however as Cases are, tho not oblig'd, We think, to accuse your self to any upon *Earth*, yet to do it before *Heaven*, and endeavor to expiate your former long habitual *lewdness* with one, and *cheat* on the other, by a continued hearty *Penitency*." (Subsequent citations of John Dunton's *Athenian Mercury* [1691–97] will identify volume, issue, and question number according to the form "*A.M.*, IX, xxviii, 2.")

discussions of matrimony.[12] In a *Supplement* to the *Review*, Defoe had pointed out to a querist that "Marriage being nothing but a Promise, the Ceremony is no Addition to the Contract, only a Thing exacted by the Law, to prevent Knaves doing what seems here to be attempted, and therefore the Society insist upon it, when the Promise was made, the Man and Woman were actually Marryed; and he can never go off from it, nor Marry any other Woman." [13] Here Moll uses similar doctrines to affect our attitude towards what she has already done, and what she is about to do. As she reiterates to the elder brother her grounds for claiming that "I am really, and in the essence of the thing, your wife" (p. 46), she makes it harder than ever for us to be severe towards her. We may not share her view that mutual consent constitutes the essence of marriage, yet we cannot deny her argument a degree of plausibility; we may recall that she was originally willing to accept her lover on any terms (or none at all), yet it now appears that she has somehow been abused. Similarly, to keep us from sympathizing with the duped younger brother at her expense, Moll suggests that she is the victim of a worse betrayal. She reminds her lover of "the long discourses you have had with me, and the many hours' pains you have taken to persuade me to believe myself an honest woman" (p. 45). Such pleas do not alter her lover's determination to palm Moll off on his

[12] See *A.M.*, VIII, iii, 1: the querist reports that *"Having for a long time pretended kindness to a Young Woman, and promis'd her Marriage if ever in a Capacity to maintain her, she thereupon yielded to my unlawful desires. Since this I'm sensible of my Crime . . . but am not yet in a capacity to live with her, tho' she's extreamly apprehensive that I'll forsake her, and I under Temptation of doing it."* He is advised that "His first Duty is, to be sure he's truly sensible of his *Crime*, and troubled for it, and endeavour to make her *Partner* in his *Repentance*, as she has bin in the *Sin*. Then we think 'tis a plain case, that he ought to *marry* her." See *A.M.*, V, ii, 4: "A publick Marriage signifies no more before God than a private Contract . . . only here's the difference, the first gives a satisfaction to the World, and renders the party proper Subjects of the Law as to Estates, *&c*." Cf. also *A.M.*, XIII, vi, 6, and XI, xxiv, 3. Among the earlier casuists, see Joseph Hall, *Resolutions and Decisions of Divers Practical Cases of Conscience*, in *Works*, ed. Philip Wynter, 10 vols. (Oxford, 1863), VII, 393–95.

[13] *Review, Supplement*, I (November, 1704), 19–20; in another *Supplement*, the querist is "oblig'd by many Engagements" to a marriage which "forshews nothing but both our Ruins," and inquires whether "I may not leave her, and try my Fortune elsewhere." In reply, Defoe's Scandal Club declares that "his promises to the young Woman cannot be so broken as to marry another, he having engaged (as he says) to marry her; which the Society always allows to be a Marriage, and cannot prevail upon themselves yet to dispense with private Contracts on future Accidents; Promises of Marriage being things not to be trifled with on any Occasion whatsoever" (I [January, 1705], 13). Four months earlier, Defoe had observed more cynically that "he that Lyes with a Woman on a promise of Matrimony, is a Knave if he does not perform his promise, and a Fool if he does" (*Review*, [I (September 5, 1704), 227]; for further discussion of this topic see Spiro Peterson, "The Matrimonial Theme of Defoe's *Roxana*," *PMLA*, LXX [1955], 180–81 and passim).

younger brother, nor do they quite persuade us that she is "an honest woman," yet they induce us to commiserate when we might otherwise condemn.

A further dimension of this episode is the elder brother's own verbal maneuvering. Among the "abundance of fine things" with which he had wooed her, he had told Moll that "though he could not mention such a thing till he came to his estate, yet he was resolved to make me happy then, and himself too; that is to say, to marry me" (pp. 28–29). To avoid baldly repudiating a promise which he has no intention of keeping, he resorts to a ruse worthy of Moll herself. In reply to her reproaches, he calmly declares, "My dear, I have not broken one promise with you yet; I did tell you I would marry you when I was come to my estate; but you see my father is a hale, healthy man, and may live these thirty years still, and not be older than several are round us in the town" (p. 45). He thus acknowledges the force of the promise, but denies that the condition for fulfilling it has been met. Moll is in one sense the victim of this evasion, but in a more important sense its beneficiary. We forget that her compliance was not grounded on the promise of marriage, and are impressed rather by the cunning that her naiveté—or at worst her folly—had to contend with.

But this is only a faint sample of the sophistry which the elder brother goes on to display in persuading Moll to accept the younger brother. This is the first of several episodes in which she eventually does something that she originally finds abhorrent, and in which her shift in attitude—from revulsion through reluctance to resigned acquiescence—is brought about by the eloquence of her advisers. Or so she means us to feel. More striking instances of this process occur later in the book, but the debate with the elder brother over marrying the younger illustrates its main outlines. Moll's summaries of the discussion convey a clear sense of her constant (though diminishing) opposition.[14] They also emphasize her antagonist's persuasive powers, for we are assured that he spoke in "much more moving terms than it is possible for me to express, and with . . . much greater force of argument than I can repeat" (p. 64). Nor does Moll make the mistake of implying that any of the elder brother's arguments are sound. When he represents to her "in lively figures" the prospect of being "turned out to the wide world a mere cast-off whore," and takes care "to lay it home to me in the worst colours that it could be possible to be drawn in," she does

---

[14] "He answered all my objections," she says, "and fortified his discourse with all the arguments that human wit and art could devise. . . . He answered all that I could object from affection, and from former engagements, with telling me the necessity that was before us of taking other measures now . . . he wrought me up, in short, to a kind of hesitation in the matter . . . Thus, in a word, I may say, he reasoned me out of my reason" (pp. 64–66).

not suggest that this is a valid argument for marrying Robin, but merely that "All this terrified me to the last degree" (p. 65). The elder brother's persuasion, she says, "at length prevailed with me to consent, though with so much reluctance, that it was easy to see I should go to church like a bear to the stake" (p. 66): the entire scene demands, in effect, who could be so heartless as to condemn the bear, which strikes out at the dogs only to defend itself. In Defoe's fiction, repudiation and denial may be almost invariable preludes to acceptance and consent. But even if we quickly surmise that the episode will end in church, we remain curious to see how Moll's sturdy reluctance can be overcome. Although the overt sophistry is all ascribed to the elder brother, the real sophist throughout the scene is Moll. One would not wish to reduce this man to a mere "projection" of the heroine, since he has an identity of his own—nameless and faceless, but no less substantial than that of any other supporting character in the book. Nonetheless one cannot help regarding him as a conveniently external prompter and apologist for Moll's behavior and thus in some sense an embodiment of one side of her total personality. Like the devil and Mother Midnight later in the book, Moll's lover expresses notions which she cannot afford to acknowledge, let alone to advocate, but which she eventually acts upon all the same.

After the marriage, Moll says of her former lover that "I committed adultery and incest with him every day in my desires, which, without doubt, was as effectually criminal in the nature of the guilt as if I had actually done it." [15] She reiterates this principle at several other points in the book; for instance, she holds that to give up one's child to a hired nurse is "an intentional murder, whether the child lives or dies." [16] *"The Intention of Murther,"* Defoe had maintained two decades earlier, *"is equally Criminal in the Eyes of God with the Act it self,"* [17] and in *Roxana*, when Amy swears that she will kill the heroine's troublesome daughter, Roxana exclaims, "why you ought to be hang'd for what you have done already; for having resolv'd on it, is

[15] P. 68; in *An Essay on the History and Reality of Apparitions* (1727), a woman is told that by loving a married man "she had intentionally committed Whoredom with him"; "you wish'd you were a-bed with him, and you are as guilty by wishing to Sin, as if you had done it" (p. 195). The Scandal Club advises one would-be adulterer "to reflect what Intentional Guilt lies on your Thoughts in this Case," and another "to repent of the sin of Adultery, since according to the known Text, *Matt.* 5:28. you have as much already committed it, as if you had actually lain together" (*Review, Supplement*, I [January, 1705], 7; I [September, 1704], 7).

[16] P. 201; cf. *Farther Adventures*, where Crusoe speaks of a "murderous intent, or to do justice to the crime, the intentional murder" (*Romances and Narratives*, II, 69).

[17] *A New Test of the Church of England's Loyalty* [1702], in *A True Collection*, p. 405; cf. *Review*, III (August 20, 1706), 400: "the Murther is already committed, and your Guilt determin'd in the Intention."

doing it, as to the Guilt of the Fact; you are a Murtherer already, as much as if you had done it already." [18]

The principle itself is not peculiar to casuistry. " 'Tis a Maxim in the Civil Law," a contemporary essayist points out, "and 'tis applicable in many Cases in the Common and Statute Laws of this Nation, and 'tis always so in the Law of God, that *Voluntas pro Facto reputatur.*" [19] But Moll's way of using this proposition is casuistical. In proclaiming that she is guilty of adultery and incest, she puts the harshest possible construction on her attachment to her first lover. Yet it is doubtful whether our response is quite as harsh as hers. First of all there is the fact that Moll is her own accuser. However culpable her desires, it is she herself who acknowledges and deplores them: the narrator's values are thus aligned with those of the respectable reader, against those of her former self. Moreover, by equating criminal desires with criminal acts, she matches even the most scrupulous reader in the rigor of his ethical standards; ostensibly an admission of frailty, Moll's remark is at the same time an assertion of moral equality. In short, Moll offers—and overtly seeks from her readers—an emphatically negative judgment of her criminal longings; nevertheless, her gesture of self-reproach may also involve an appeal to our fellow-feeling.

Whatever our response to this particular confession, it is part of a larger strategy that clearly tends to her advantage. Here Moll maintains, seemingly against her own interest, that wicked desires are "as effectually criminal" as wicked deeds. If we accept this view, we are apt to acquiesce in a doctrine that is implicit and crucial in much of what she says of herself: namely that innocent desires are as effectually virtuous as innocent deeds. On this occasion she candidly concedes that her outward virtue belies her true guilt; many other episodes make the point that her outward guilt belies her true virtue. I have already noted the passage in which an "intentional" marriage is held to be as "effectual" as a public ceremony, and although the terminology elsewhere in the book is often less explicit, the role of motive or purpose remains crucial. "A Good Intention," says Addison, "joined to an Evil Action, extenuates its Malignity, and in some cases may take it wholly away";[20]

[18] P. 273; Defoe makes a similar point in the *Serious Reflections,* where he argues that "a vicious inclination removed from the object is still a vicious inclination, and contracts the same guilt as if the object were at hand; . . . it is true, separating the man from the object is the way to make any act impossible to be committed, yet . . . the guilt does not lie in the act only, but in the intention or desire to commit it" (*Romances and Narratives,* III, 8). Cf. *Applebee's Journal* for March 11, 1721 (Lee, II, 350), and *The Perjur'd Free Mason Detected* (1730), pp. 10, 22.

[19] Whitelock Bulstrode, *Essays upon the Following Subjects* (1724), p. 126.

[20] *The Spectator,* No. 213 (November 3, 1711), ed. Donald F. Bond, 5 vols. (Oxford, 1965), II, 331. " 'Tis a kind of good Action to mean well, and the Intention ought to palliate the Failure," Defoe says in *Augusta Triumphans* (1728), p. 3; in *More Ref-*

it is towards this principle, so essential to Moll's pleas for sympathy, that even her confession of adulterous desires paradoxically points.

Moll describes her second spouse, a linen-draper, as "this land-water thing called a gentleman-tradesman" (p. 70); soon after their marriage, she reports that "my new husband coming to a lump of money at once, fell into . . . a profusion of expense," and a case of conscience arises over the course a wife should follow when her husband's extravagances threaten family ruin. Or rather, Moll once again finds herself in a predicament that corresponds to a traditional case of conscience, but responds to it in a manner which has little to do with conscience. When the man is finally arrested for debt, Moll says that "It was no surprise to me, for I had foreseen some time that all was going to wreck, and had been taking care to reserve something if I could, though it was not much, for myself" (p. 72). The Athenian Society, in response to an inquiry whether such practices are justifiable, had maintained that "in some Cases such secret securing one parties separate interest, without giving the other any account, may be very just, vertuous, and prudent. As for Instance, when either the Man or the Wife run on willfully and obstinately in an unavoidable Course of ruining themselves and their Families . . . all convenient tenderness, Admonition and Counsel . . . ought to be made use of; which if to no purpose, the last Remedy is as reasonable as to lay things of value out of the way of Children and Fools." [21] Moll takes this doctrine so much for granted that she feels no need to defend her action; if "all [is] going to wreck," it is clearly better to conduct salvage operations beforehand than afterwards.

Once the remaining goods have become the legal property of her husband's creditors, however, Moll cannot so easily escape the moral implications of salvaging them for herself.[22] Without denying that the act itself is culpable, she concentrates on the question of responsibility for it. Her husband, she says, "would have me go home, and in the

---

ormation [1703], he says "If thou hast err'd, tho' with a good Intent,/ One merits Pity, t'other Punishment" (in *A Second Volume Of The Writings Of The Author Of The True-Born Englishman* [1705], p. 57). For "intention" used to aggravate rather than lighten a misdeed, cf. also *Conjugal Lewdness* (1727), where contraception is held to be as bad as abortion, since they "are equally wicked in their Intention, and it is the End of everything, that makes it Good or Evil" (p. 139).

[21] *A.M.*, V, ix, 2; cf. *A.M.*, IX, xiv, 9, and William Ames, *Conscience with the Power and the Cases thereof* (1643), p. 206.

[22] In answer to a debtor's question *"Whether it be Lawful to run to . . . priviledged places* [such as the Mint] *for protection"* the Athenian Society points out that "there's difference between getting out of the way ones self, and carrying off Effects and Goods . . . which are none of our own . . . One of the vilest sort of Knaveries, and in some Sence worse than *Publick Robbery* . . . Of t'other side, it must be own'd *every thing wou'd fain live,* and 'tis a *severe Tryal* of a mans *Honesty* to give that out of his *Hands,* which shou'd keep him from *Starving."* (*A.M.*, XII, xxiv, 2).

night take away everything I had in the house of any value, and secure it" (p. 72). Any suspicion that Moll might have done the same thing on her own initiative is thus forestalled by labeling the act his suggestion. Moreover, Moll acknowledges the fact of the theft in such a way as to shift its onus to him: "He used me very handsomely and with good manners upon all occasions, even to the last, only spent all I had, and left me to rob the creditors for something to subsist on" (Ibid.). Moll does not rob the creditors of her own volition, but is "left" to rob them by her husband: the parallel phrases "[he] spent all I had, and [he] left me to rob the creditors" again suggest that she is a mere tool, more victim than villain. Similarly, the final "for something to subsist on" introduces a further extenuation: Moll is prompted not only by her husband's counsel, but by her own necessity.

"My condition was very odd," Moll says at the end of this episode, "for . . . I was a widow bewitched; I had a husband and no husband, and I could not pretend to marry again, though I knew well enough my husband would never see England any more, if he lived fifty years. Thus, I say, I was limited from marriage, what offer soever might be made me; and I had not one friend to advise with in the condition I was in." [23] One noteworthy feature of this passage is the "husband and no husband" paradox, which will complicate Moll's subsequent marriages. Moreover, she will more than once become involved with men who have "a wife and no wife," so that the ambiguities of her own situation will be compounded by those of the people she moves among. Another point is her lack of "one friend to advise with": she must make her own way through the wilderness of matrimonial casuistry. Each of these factors tends to make us less severe towards her subsequent matrimonial ventures than we might be if her status was altogether clear, or there was anyone trustworthy at hand to clarify it for her.[24] Moll never denies that she remains married, in the eyes of English law, to the gentleman-tradesman who has absconded, but at opportune moments her odd husband-and-no-husband condition allows her to overlook this inconvenient fact. And she contrives to make us overlook it as well: for instance, the next episode opens with the statement, "I had made an acquaintance with a very sober, good sort of a woman, who was a widow, too, like me" (p. 76). The final three

---

[23] P. 74; see Defoe's lengthy discussion of the similar case of a "Widower Bewich'd" in the "Advice from the Scandal Club" (*Review*, II [April 24, 1705], 86–88).

[24] Had she had access to the Athenian Society or Scandal Club, Moll need not have felt so keenly the lack of a friend's advice, since those learned bodies were familiar with her predicament. For an involved query, the gist of which is *"whether it is not the same thing in the sight of God (in this Woman's case) as tho' her Husband were really dead"*—so that the woman may proceed as if she were a widow—see *A.M.*, III, xix, 1.

words, and others equally unobtrusive elsewhere, help to make plausible Moll's widowhood, by dint of casual iteration if not of legal argument; or at least they make us less censorious than we would be if we found her deliberately hypocritical about her marital status.[25]

In the episode that follows, Moll's own memoir comes to a standstill as she tells the story of the courtship and marriage of her next-door neighbor. Previous critics have noted that these pages touch on a topic recurrent in Defoe's writings—the hazards and hardships that marriage holds for women; nevertheless the episode has been treated as a narrative digression, an extended anecdote with little bearing on Moll's own character or actions. But the episode is built loosely around a case of conscience which Moll is soon to face: namely, the question of whether it is legitimate to deceive a deceiver. Elsewhere Defoe was to cite "the old Latin Proverb, *Fallere fallentem non est fraus,* (which Men construe, or rather Render, by way of banter upon Satan) 'tis no Sin to cheat the *Devil,* which for all that, upon the whole I deny." [26] Here Defoe's answer to the question is negative, yet his heroine is about to respond with an implicit affirmative. He thus has a fresh opportunity to demonstrate the casuistical theorem that circumstances alter cases. To deceive a would-be deceiver is ordinarily a bad thing, but it may under special conditions become understandable and hence pardonable, if not commendable.

For Moll the actual question is whether, since "the men made no scruple to set themselves out as persons meriting a woman of fortune, when they had really no fortune of their own," it would be "just to deal with them in their own way" (p. 89). Through the tale of her

---

[25] The reviewer of a recent book says that "its author can be excused of dishonesty only on the grounds that before deceiving others he has taken great pains to deceive himself"; and a recent commentator says of Moll Flanders that "she deceives herself, but is unaware that she is doing so." Moll's claims to widowhood would certainly be open to one charge or the other, were it not for the fact that her position is genuinely ambiguous. (P. B. Medawar, *The Art of the Soluble* [1967], p. 71; Bonamy Dobrée, Introduction to World's Classics *Moll Flanders*, p. vi).

[26] *Political History of the Devil* (1726), p. 353. On the question, *"Whether it be a Sin to deceive the Deceiver?"* see *A.M.*, II, xx, 10, where it is pointed out that "although Circumstances may make an Action more or less sinful, yet they change not the nature of Sin; for Deceit is Deceit, though used to a Deceiver." On the other hand, the notorious Mary Carleton had appealed to her readers "whether, being prompted by such plain and public signs of a design upon me, to counterplot them I have done any more than what . . . a received principle of justice directs: 'to deceive the deceiver is no deceit' " (Francis Kirkman, *The Counterfeit Lady Unveiled* [1673], ed. Spiro Peterson [Garden City, 1951], p. 23). Similarly, "Tom a Bedlam" argues in *Applebee's Journal* that *"fallere fallentem non est fraus; or, in English, 'Tis no Sin to Cheat the Devil' "* (April 7, 1722; Lee, II, 508); and in *Amusements Serious and Comical* (1700), Tom Brown (mistakenly) declares, "All our casuists agree that it is no more sin to cheat a Jew than to over-reach a Scot, or to put false dice upon a stock jobber" (ed. Arthur L. Hayward [1927], p. 200).

neighbor, Moll establishes that London marriages were "the consequences of political schemes for forming interests, and carrying on
business"; that "the market ran very unhappily on the men's side;"
that "the men had such choice everywhere, that the case of the women
was very unhappy"; and particularly that "the men made no scruple
. . . to go a-fortune hunting, as they call it, when they had really no
fortune themselves to demand it, or merit to deserve it" (pp. 77, 78).
These remarks echo Defoe's lamentations elsewhere over the crassness
of contemporary match-making, and over the resulting indignity and
injustice to women. Here, however, Moll's comments have the more
immediate purpose of generating sympathy towards anything, however
drastic, abused women may resort to in self-defense. She does not intro-
duce these data to extenuate any action of her own: she presents them
as casual reflections on the experience of her neighbor, and the air of
disinterestedness not only helps to persuade us of their validity, but
prevents us from suspecting that Moll is up to some anticipatory plead-
ing in her own behalf.

Under Moll's guidance, "this young lady played her part so well,
that . . . she made [her suitor's] obtaining her be to him the most
difficult thing in the world" (p. 84). "This she did," Moll goes on to
say, ". . . by a just policy, turning the tables upon him, and playing
back upon him his own game." The language of playing parts, turning
tables and playing games prevents our weighing this woman's actions
too gravely, and makes us assent the more easily to the "justice" of her
"policy." Part of Moll's task is to make such practices seem as in-
nocuous as possible, which she achieves through metaphors of acting
and gaming suggestive of Restoration comedy. Another part of her
task, though, is to establish the parallel between her case and the other
woman's: if we approve of her friend's table-turning, we are likely to
condone her own version as well. These pages are therefore anything
but a digression. They are an indispensable prelude to Moll's account
of her matrimonial parleying with the Virginia planter, in that they
furnish prior justification for what she is about to do.

Moll also seeks to lessen her responsibility for this venture by por-
traying herself once more as a passive tool of others' cunning. "My
intimate friend," she reports, "whom I had so faithfully served in her
case with the captain . . . was as ready to serve me" (p. 88). This
woman, whom Moll also refers to as "my dear and faithful friend" and
"a steady friend to me," proposes that she try to "deceive the deceiver";
after loading her with such epithets, how could Moll question her
advice? Left to herself, Moll suggests, she would never have thought
of such a scheme, or managed to carry it out. "The captain's lady, in
short, put this project into my head, and told me if I would be ruled
by her I should certainly get a husband . . . I told her . . . that I

would give up myself wholly to her directions, and that I would have neither tongue to speak nor feet to step in that affair but as she should direct me, depending that she would extricate me out of every difficulty." [27] In fact, Moll needs no assistance whatever: after all, she had "faithfully served" the captain's lady in the first place by proposing (in Rochester's words) that she "revenge herself on her undoer, Man" (p. 84). The passage makes sense only if we regard it as another piece of determined self-justification, and in any case the sense it makes is rhetorical rather than logical. The preceding episode sought to establish that it is legitimate for women to turn the tables on men. This passage, on the other hand, implies that the forthcoming attempt to turn the tables on men may be culpable, but that the fault is not Moll's but her friend's. The object is not consistency but comprehensiveness. [28]

Moll's ruse to obtain a husband clearly involves deception, but its ethical status is complicated by two subordinate issues, each of which has a history of its own in the literature of casuistry. In the first place, can one be guilty of lying without uttering a single untruth? And secondly, can one be guilty of lying through speaking literal truths? The two questions are closely related, and the traditional answers to

[27] When the middle-aged Moll uses makeup for the first time, she protests that "I had never yielded to the baseness of paint before" (p. 217). Bonamy Dobrée says of "yielded" that "the word is perfectly chosen" (Introduction, p. ix), and one cannot help agreeing; yet it should be noted that this is one of Moll's favorite formulas for suggesting her passive or reluctant role in mischief of all kinds. Early in the book she declares to her seducer that "I have yielded to the importunities of my affection" (p. 46); later she assures the gentleman at Bath that their becoming lovers had been "all a surprise, and was owing to the accident of our having yielded too far to our mutual inclinations" (p. 138); and when she has become a hardened thief, and can no longer allege that poverty or the devil prompts her to continue "this horrid trade," she speaks of herself as "yielding to the importunities of my crime" (p. 239). If Fielding had written the book, one could speak confidently of "yielding" as an ironic motif, especially since other characters play on the word wittily: "They that yield when they're asked," Robin taunts his eldest sister in the Colchester household, "are one step before them that were never asked to yield, sister, and two steps before them that yield before they are asked" (p. 51). But with Defoe, as Dobrée observes elsewhere, "one never quite knows" ("Some Aspects of Defoe's Prose," in *Pope and His Contemporaries: Essays Presented to George Sherburn*, ed. James L. Clifford and Louis A. Landa [Oxford, 1949], p. 177). "Our interest in [*Moll Flanders*]," Wayne Booth rightly observes, "depends on decisions which even now, more than two hundred years after the event, cannot be made with any assurance" (*The Rhetoric of Fiction* [Chicago, 1961], p. 322).

[28] Moll's tactics somewhat resemble those in the following story: "A. borrowed a copper kettle from B. and after he returned it was sued by B. because the kettle now had a big hole in it which made it unusable. His defense was: 'First, I never borrowed a kettle from B. at all; secondly, the kettle had a hole in it already when I got it from him; and thirdly, I gave him back the kettle undamaged'" (Sigmund Freud, *Jokes and their Relation to the Unconscious* [1905], in *Complete Psychological Works*, ed. James Strachey [1960], VIII, 62).

both had been emphatically affirmative;[29] nevertheless Moll speaks and acts on the assumption that each should be answered in the negative. The Virginia planter courts her "upon supposition . . . that I was very rich, though I never told him a word of it myself" (p. 90); by avoiding overt misrepresentation, Moll feels that she escapes responsibility for the man's error. A bolder stroke is the exchange of verses, in which she expresses literal truths with the intention of being disbelieved. In response to the man's "I scorn your gold, and yet I love," Moll writes "I'm poor: let's see how kind you'll prove," and adds the ingenuous comment, "This was a sad truth to me; whether he believed me or no, I could not tell; I supposed then that he did not." [30] Moll concludes that "though I had jested with him (as he supposed it) so often about my poverty, yet when he found it to be true, he had foreclosed all manner of objection, seeing whether . . . I was in jest or in earnest, I had declared myself to be very poor . . . and though he might say afterwards he was cheated, yet he could never say that I cheated him" (pp. 92–93). What must be noted here is not simply that Moll's argument is specious, although generations of casuists had insisted that such reasoning sacrifices the spirit of truth to the letter, but that it is just plausible enough to prevent her husband, when he finally learns the facts, from being indignant towards her. "I have no reason to blame you," he assures Moll; "I may perhaps tell the captain [who officiously spread the rumor of her fortune] he has cheated me, but I can never say you have cheated me" (p. 96). Such is "his affection to [Moll], and the goodness of his temper" (p. 92) that he does not reproach her—yet he, after all, is the injured party. His benign response serves as a model for ours, and this seems to be the real point of these passages. Their object is not to gain our assent but our indulgence, and the husband's exemplary tolerance contributes to this effect as surely, if not as strikingly, as Moll's own ventures into verse and her accompanying rationalizations.

After Moll has taken such pains to offset the potential severity of our judgment, the following statement seems strangely at odds with the

[29] On these questions, see Taylor, *Ductor Dubitantium*, in *Whole Works*, X, 128–30, 106–10; Richard Baxter, *Christian Directory*, in *Practical Works*, ed. William Orme, 23 vols. (1830), III, 512.

[30] Moll prefaces her final rhyme by saying, "I ventured all upon the last cast of poetry": again the imagery of gambling allows her to sustain the excitement of the encounter, and yet to dispel its somberer implications with the pretence that it is all a civilized game. Robert Alter remarks that Moll's "variety of extralegal activities is not in the least a game for her; on the contrary, she envisages virtually everything she does as a very serious business" (*Rogue's Progress: Studies in the Picaresque Novel* [Cambridge, Mass., 1964], pp. 46–47). Broadly speaking this is so, and makes Moll's use of game-motifs to keep *us* from regarding her deception as "a very serious business" all the more noteworthy.

rest of her defense: "I often reflected on myself how doubly criminal it was to deceive such a man; but that necessity, which pressed me to a settlement suitable to my condition, was my authority for it" (p. 92). Instead of denying the gravity of her deception, Moll here acknowledges it to the full; as on other occasions, her own sternness seems calculated to forestall ours.[31] At this point Moll wisely avoids dwelling on the "authority" of "necessity"; whatever its intrinsic validity, the plea of necessity will not bear close scrutiny in the present context. Yet the allusion to necessity plays its part, together with all the other lines of defense. Analyzed individually, none of Moll's arguments will exonerate her, and collectively they form a curious web of contradiction and inconsistency. To prevent our pausing to examine them singly *or* collectively, however, Moll presents her brief at a brisk pace. "It is well to expand the argument and insert things that it does not require at all," says Cicero, "for in the multitude of details the whereabouts of the fallacy is obscured"; and it is well, Moll might have added, to be quick about it, too.

[31] "He is extremely ready to own his errors," Clarissa says of Lovelace, "By this means, silencing by acknowledgment the objections he cannot answer; which may give him the praise of ingenuousness, when he can obtain no other; . . . He knows . . . that his own wild pranks cannot be concealed; and so owns just enough to palliate (because it teaches you not to be surprised at) any new one, that may come to your ears; and then, truly, he is, however faulty, a mighty ingenuous man; and by no means an *hypocrite*" (*Clarissa*, 9 vols. [Oxford, 1930], I, 295, II, 150). There is something of the same artful candor about Moll.

Between the Real and the Moral: Problems in the Structure of *Moll Flanders*

by *Lee Edwards*

Professor Eucalyptus said, "The search
For reality is as momentous as
The search for god."

—Wallace Stevens, *An Ordinary
Evening in New Haven*

That the structure of *Moll Flanders* should raise critical problems is not surprising in view of the tasks Defoe set for himself in the Preface to that work. In it he claims that his book will be an example of the good and the true; significantly, however, he does not claim for it the status of the beautiful. The difficulties involved in harmonizing a concern with moral persuasiveness with a concern with literal authenticity had vexed English prose fiction writers since at least the Elizabethan era. The resolution of this problem—the ability to display the two interests simultaneously and in terms of each other, rather than at each other's expense—is a singularly important transition in the development of prose fiction. The obvious question, then: Does Defoe demonstrate in *Moll Flanders* that he possesses the technical resources to harmonize these two concerns or do they finally work at cross-purposes throughout the book, so that the end result is a work which is neither ironic nor ambiguous, as many have claimed, but simply unresolved? [1]

In attempting to answer this question, I would suggest that we begin by accepting Defoe's Preface as a guide to the meaning of *Moll Flanders* in order to see if we can find that his statements there have

---

"Between the Real and the Moral: Problems in the Structure of Moll Flanders*"
by Lee R. Edwards. Copyright © by Prentice-Hall, Inc. This essay is printed here
for the first time.*

[1] A great deal of critical energy has been spent, especially of late, trying to answer this question. For a good review of the bulk of this recent critical literature see Ian Watt, "The Recent Critical Fortunes of *Moll Flanders*," *Eighteenth-Century Studies*, I (1967), 109–26.

particular, specifiable consequences for the structure of the book as a whole. As we have noted, Defoe tells us that we are primarily meant to be morally edified by what we will read. We should learn to praise "diligence and application . . . and an unwearied industry," to condemn "foolish, thoughtless, and abhor'd conduct," and to see that men are "unable . . . to preserve the most solemn resolutions of virtue without divine assistance." If it were true that Defoe made these solemn assurances, the same ones with which Moll provides us in the work itself, with a large piece of tongue in his cheek, then one might expect the book itself to present some evidence of this ironic stance. Possibly, the structure of the work as a whole might be made to put pressure on Moll's views, to reveal them as wrong, hypocritical, or not productive of success. Alternatively, we might be made to dislike Moll herself.[2] Or, finally, a character might emerge who would verbally disqualify the attitude expressed in the Preface, who would show that, contrary to what was originally stated, traditional Christianity does not provide an adequate framework for the economically expanding universe of the early eighteenth century.

Although to my knowledge no critic has in fact suggested that such an explosion of Christian values might be among Defoe's purposes in writing *Moll Flanders,* I do not believe that raising this possibility creates a pseudoproblem where none really exists. On the contrary, this view seems to me to be simply a logical extension of one which is currently common: that is, while Moll is a character whom we like and of whose methods we approve, our evaluation of her is in terms which vitiate the Christian strictures with which she is surrounded. Thus if our blessing of Moll is not in the language of the traditional Christian beatitudes, then we ought at least to consider the possibility that the invocation of this language within the book is meant as an ironic devaluation not of the character mouthing the pieties, but of the pieties themselves. While it certainly does not appear that *Moll Flanders* represents Defoe's attempt to work out this ironic possibility, any consideration of the work as one whose predominant mode is irony ought, I think, to be aware of its potentially two-edged nature.

However the task is managed, if we are meant either to condemn or to view ironically the version of the Christian ethic proffered by both Moll and Defoe, then it seems reasonable to expect that one of these three alternatives would be chosen: either the book must overtly shift

---

[2] Swift, in *A Modest Proposal,* creates a supremely ironic work in which two of the three conditions here proposed are not met. Although counter arguments are presented, the Projector ostensibly demolishes them and seems about to be rewarded by unleashing his fiendish appetite on a series of helpless infants. Swift's irony, however, is in large measure created as a product of the unchecked animosity which the reader is allowed to feel toward the speaker.

its moral stance; or Moll must be punished in some way for holding the view she does; or the reader's feelings for Moll must be at least equivocal, if not wholly negative. But Defoe avails himself of none of these alternatives. No character speaks out against either Moll or her religion. Far from being punished, Moll is rewarded for her views. And to dislike the character Moll Flanders is to dislike the whole book of which she is the heroine.[3] Thus it is hard to see how we can take ironically the suggestions for the reading of the work that are offered at its opening.

The book is structurally complicated, however, because if we cannot condemn or even distance ourselves from Moll's morality, neither can we wholly accept it. Defoe has, it seems, attempted to provide a single perspectival framework, that of Christianity, to contain a narrative structure which he says is patterned on the events of a real life. What happens, however, is that the narrative demands its own very different perspective—one which glorifies resourcefulness and vitality in the face of the pressure of necessity. Responding to the narrative alone, the reader tends either to judge Moll in terms of her own Christian strictures and find her wanting or to judge Christianity in terms of Moll's abundant vitality and find it lifeless and inadequate. In either case, the reality with which Defoe's narrative, in distinction from his Preface, is primarily concerned is incompatible with the Christian precepts originally proposed to contain it. Yet neither the narrative nor the morality which frames it responds to the pressures which the other is exerting. Far from being productive of a fruitful ironic tension, the opposition between the real and the moral in *Moll Flanders* is productive only of wobble.

The overall structure of the book is troubled as much by these perspectival problems as it is by difficulties concerning the shape of the narrative alone. In terms of purely narrative structure, in fact, the sequence of events which makes up Moll's life is tighter than it is sometimes given credit for being. Moll moves over a vast terrain of time and space, abandoning a profuse number of husbands, lovers, and children in her wake. But her path from Newgate to Colchester, Bath, London, America, Lancashire, London, Colchester, Newgate, America, England does exhibit a satisfying circularity in its overall pattern,[4]

[3] See, for example, Mark Schorer, "Technique as Discovery," *Hudson Review*, I (1948), 67–87.

[4] See Terence Martin, "The Unity of *Moll Flanders*," *MLQ*, XXII (1961), 115–24. This article is primarily devoted to showing "a pattern in the structural counterpart of Moll Flander's interior existence . . ." (p. 123). Martin's secondary thesis, however, seems a bit overingenious. He states that Moll's stealing, particularly of watches, in the second part of the book is psychologically related to her compulsive marrying in the first part, that theft represents Moll's attempt both to recover her lost fertility and to show a capitalist society that she is still a productive entity.

even though at any given moment we are in doubt about the particular incidents the next pages will dramatize. This doubt, which is the structural flaw most often pointed to, arises because the goal which Moll has set herself (or which Defoe has set for her), is not realized in terms of the resolution of a single narrative action. Moll's end—the one she sets herself as a charity-orphan in Colchester—is to be a gentle-woman (itself susceptible of ironic interpretation, as Moll learns to her own chagrin) and to avoid being left alone. Insofar as the book has a pattern of action, this pattern involves Moll's search for the protection afforded by the presence of either money or a man or, preferably, both.

Richardson, writing *Pamela* some twenty years later, created a heroine whose position in the world and whose personal aims were similar to Moll's. But Richardson solved the problem of narrative and perspectival structure by means of an innovation in the techniques available for writing the long prose fiction. Instead of simply keeping the final goal constant while tracing out the means to it with the infinite variety admitted to by Defoe and his predecessors, Richardson made the successful fulfillment of his heroine's destiny hinge upon the final resolution of one set of narrative and personal conflicts, the relationship between Pamela and Squire B. Pamela's marriage to B. means her success as both a moral being and a social agent, while any other resolution of the plot would have meant the inevitable failure to attain one of these goals. Richardson could have arranged the final disposition of events in ways other than he did: he could have had B. rape Pamela, or Pamela could have been made to return to her parents. But her failure to attain an honorable marriage with B. would un-equivocally, as the value system of the book is constructed, have had to imply her failure in the moral and/or social spheres as well.[5] Because modern audiences generally fail to value virginity as highly as either Richardson or his heroine did, some readers see *Pamela* in the same ironic light by which they read *Moll Flanders* and find it an unwitting exposure of the hypocrisy behind the pious platitude. But there is no doubt that, overtly at least, Pamela has resolutely refused to compromise her moral integrity. The events of the narrative and the espoused morality coincide rather than conflict.

Because Defoe modelled his narrative on the more traditional pattern for prose fiction, the simple sequence, the surface of *Moll Flanders* does not have the cumulative power that Richardson's work demonstrates. It does, however, reveal some attempt on Defoe's part to control the grosser vagaries of the popular genres. Thus Defoe entirely sup-

[5] Richardson explores such a seeming failure in *Clarissa*. But the values which allow the heroine of the later book to emerge triumphant are much more complex than any introduced in *Pamela*.

presses the history of Jemmy, the Lancashire husband, and reduces the history of the governess to a portion of a paragraph:

> My good old governess, to give a short touch at her history, tho' she had left off the trade, was, as I may say, born a pick-pocket, and, as I understood afterward, had run thro' all the several degrees of that art, and yet had been taken but once; when she was so grossly detected, that she was convicted and order'd to be transported; but being a woman of a rare tongue, and withal having money in her pocket, she found means, the ship putting into Ireland for provisions, to get on shore there, where she practiced her old trade some years; when falling into another sort of company she turned midwife and procuress, and play'd a hundred pranks, which she gave me a little history of, in confidence between us as we grew more intimate. . . .

Any experience with other criminal biographies, English picaresque adventures such as those written by Kirkman and Head, or even romances, would lead us to expect that the lives of these two figures, both of whom are so important to Moll, would have been blown up into full-scale histories with each of the governess's "hundred pranks" receiving individual mention instead of being so tactfully attenuated. In addition, some of those adventures which are treated at length— Moll's various affairs and marriages with the Colchester brothers, the man from Bath, the London banker—are handled with a fair degree of emotional and narrative complexity. Moreover, the sequences dealing with Moll's incestuous marriage, as well as her marriage to Jemmy and her relationship to her governess, have consequences which act as determinants for the large scale structure of the book.

Undermining such strength, however, is Defoe's inability or unwillingness to provide a total structure which would allow us to know at any given point where Moll is in relation to her goal and what the likely consequences of each act might involve. It is true that Moll's prospects reach their nadir when she is in Newgate, under threat of hanging, and move from that point upward with her rediscovery of Jemmy, her relatively unselfish love of him, and their transportation together to America where they are finally able to establish themselves as gentlefolk in a new society which neither holds them responsible for past sins nor forces them to commit new ones. This relatively tight structure, however, occupies only one-fifth of the book, and for the rest it is hard to see that either Moll's various sexual relationships or her various felonies mark any very systematic progress to perdition. Is bigamy worse than incest? Is stealing an untended bundle containing "a suit of child-bed linnen . . . , a silver porringer . . . , a small silver mug and six spoons, with some other linnen, a good smock, and three silk hankerchiefs, and in the mug, in a paper, eighteen shillings and six-pence in money" less criminal than taking "a gold watch, with a silk purse of gold, [a] fine full bottom perewig, and silver fring'd gloves, [a] sword, and fine snuff-box"? Thus though the narrative in large traces the corruption of a human being, initially under the pressures of poverty and solitude and later under the mounting power of corruption itself, it is hard to see this control operating in small to relate the individual episodes to one another. While each of the various parts in the book is related to Moll's desire to become a gentlewoman, a status associated in her mind with freedom from economic want, the whole has finally the power of accumulation rather than that of dovetailed construction. Variety rather than unity is Defoe's self-proclaimed aim, and *Moll Flanders,* while not a wholly wild narrative, is nonetheless still feral.

Despite these flaws, however, *Moll Flanders* actually does represent a step forward in the possibilities of coherent narrative structure, unified partly, as we have seen, by a circular pattern of events and partly in terms of the causal relationships among these events. Because Moll would be a gentlewoman, she must try to marry well; because one of her husbands has a plantation in Virginia, she goes to America; because her husband turns out to be her brother, she must leave America; because she is growing old and less desirable, she replaces illicit sexual activities with theft as a means of gaining the money she needs; because she is caught stealing, she goes to Newgate; because she is in Newgate, she can be plausibly reunited with the one former husband she loves and whose position in relation to the world most closely parallels her own; because a possible punishment for crime is transportation, she and Jemmy can be sent back to America, where the two are able at last to reach their goal and enjoy respectable middle-class life. These evident causal connections, though they by no means encompass every scene in the book, do provide a skeleton for its rather too well-padded body.

If Defoe partially succeeded in imposing a measure of coherence upon the chaos of life, did he similarly succeed in even partially controlling our attitudes toward the events which make up this life? Even more germane is the question of the simultaneity or lack of it between the perception of a particular event and the formation of an attitude toward it. No reader or viewer of *Macbeth,* for example, can witness the murder of Duncan without a feeling of horror and revulsion. The event is not simply Duncan's murder, but Duncan's hideous murder, which brings retribution with it and which damns its perpetrator; the attitude which we are expected to take toward the deed is implicit in the language and atmosphere which surround it. Gesture and meaning are one. That the same is not true of *Moll Flanders* is evident. And in the gap between event and meaning the structure of *Moll Flanders* founders.

The presence of this gap can be seen in even a cursory examination of some aspects of Defoe's technique. In the first place, as Defoe in his Preface separates his moral from his fable, so in the book as a whole are the passages of moral evaluation separated from the presentation of the incident itself. Defoe's fidelity to the formal commitment implied in the notion that *Moll Flanders* is an authentic piece of nonfiction prevents him from making these comments in his own voice; Moll herself must always evaluate her own actions. Since most of these actions are criminal, difficulties immediately arise. How can the sinner expect to be believed if she condemns her acts and repents of them even as she is about to go out and sin again? There is a distinction to be made here between psychological ambivalence and perspectival clarity. On the one hand, it is both psychologically natural and narratively acceptable for a character to rationalize his own actions, to fail to realize the forces which truly govern his behavior. On the other hand, however, the author must make clear, by structural and stylistic manipulations, that his character either is or is not lying to himself. While it is not necessary for a character always to understand his motivations, it is desirable for a reader to have this information. Failure to gain this knowledge leads a reader not to distrust the character, but to distrust the book and the author who created it.

Secondly, whereas it is possible to make an event vivid simply by accumulating enough data concerning its externals, a religious or emotional experience can only be evaluated in the recreation of a moment of perception. A failure to create belief in the process of perception is a failure to create belief in the perception itself. Thirdly, that the events are presented at much greater length and with much more detail than are the "morals" suggests that Defoe's capabilities, if not his intentions, inclined him to be more at home with external action than with internal process: we learn a great deal about what is involved in arranging a bigamous marriage or providing for the birth of a child, but very little about what it feels like to regret abandoning this same husband or child when necessity calls. For example, when Moll has been abandoned for the first time by Jemmy, she recounts her reaction:

> Nothing that ever befel me in my life sunk so deep into my heart as this farewel. I reproach'd him a thousand times in my thoughts for leaving me, for I would have gone with him thro' the world, if I had beg'd my bread. I felt in my pocket and there I found the guineas, his gold watch, and two little rings, one a small diamond ring, worth only about six pounds, and the other a plain gold ring.
>
> I sat down and look'd upon these things two hours together, and scarce spoke a word, till my maid interrupted me by telling me my dinner was ready.

While there is no reason to doubt Moll's statement that she feels grief, we cannot feel the magnitude of her sorrow, sandwiched as it is between his jewelry and her dinner.

Finally, and perhaps most importantly, the kind of interest provoked by Moll's account of the various events of her life simply does not seem to be compatible with the kind of moral vision which is then imposed. For example, the language Moll uses to describe the final break with her Bath lover is revealing. When Moll talks of being "abandon'd by heaven," being "cast off," being "a single person . . . loos'd from all the obligations . . . in the world," and having "the world to begin again," these relatively explicit Christian terms gain a certain resonance because of their context. After all, Moll has been repenting:

> I then reproach'd my self with the liberties I had taken, and how I had been a snare to this gentleman, and that indeed I was principal in the crime; that now he was mercifully snatch'd out of the gulph by a convincing work upon his mind . . . .

and repenting:

> I cannot but reflect upon the unhappy consequences of too great freedoms between persons slated as we were, upon the pretence of innocent intentions, love of friendship, and the like; for the flesh has generally so great a share in these friendships that it is great odds but inclination prevails at last over the most solemn resolutions; and that vice breaks in at the breaches of decency, which really innocent friendship ought to preserve with the greatest strictness.

But the reverberations are destroyed even as they are created, as Moll overbalances the moral abstractions with the freight of the secular world. In a wholly Christian world, the poor and solitary individual has the greatest potential for closeness to God: this potentiality is what Moll's language seems to be striving to create. In Moll's world, however, the plight of the Christian, particularly when this figure is herself, can be solved only in practical terms. Thus, because Moll's knowledge that she has sinned does not tell her how she is to maintain herself in the world, she blames heaven for forcing her to "a continuing in . . . wickedness." Her solitude and freedom from obligations turn out to be associated not with the freedom of the Christian pilgrim to turn to God, but rather with Moll's quite literal and physical freedom to "finally marry again to whom I pleas'd." And, having the world to begin again means not that Moll is reborn into a life of Christian purity, but that she must provide for her future state of life, considering always that she "was not the same woman as . . . liv'd at Rotherhigh; for . . . there would always be some difference seen between five-and-twenty and two-and-forty."

In analytic terms, then, *Moll Flanders* represents an attempt on Defoe's part to solve a rather complex problem in perspectival structure: the repentant Moll must tell the story of the unrepentant Moll in such a way that we know both that the events with which she is for the most part dealing constitute her life in a state of sin and that she has ultimately said her *mea culpa* or the Protestant equivalent. Had Defoe delayed all mention of Moll's repentance until the Newgate scenes, his vivid recreations of a life of vice and crime could easily have been made compatible with his declared moral aim; he could have demonstrated both the forces that impel a being to sin and the possibility of final repentance. But the solution that he did choose, while more complex, is, as he develops it, counterproductive. Instead of widening the Christian moral framework so that it could fully contain Moll's narrative of sin, Defoe tries to yoke the two elements together. Moll is repeatedly both sinner and penitent throughout the book. While this vision is easily rendered as an icon—for a single frozen moment—it proves impossible for Defoe to sustain in repetition.

The critic, however, cannot avoid the problems posed by Defoe's double perspective by simplifying the book. The matrix around which *Moll Flanders* is built is not the single one implied in calling it a "spiritual autobiography" any more than is the single one implied in the term true history. G. A. Starr, who claims that many of Defoe's works fall within the former category, describes it as follows:

> Spiritual autobiography pursued thematic coherence amid or despite narrative incoherence: incoherence, that is, measured by the more rigorous standards of plotting which the novel was to evolve. So long as the protagonist's inward vicissitudes obeyed the traditional pattern either of growth or decay, and so long as individual episodes contributed to this pattern with some consistency, an autobiography might be regarded as structurally sound. Within such a convention, whose rationale lay in religious psychology rather than aesthetics, a logic of spiritual change within the character took precedence over a logic of outward action; within such a convention, discrete, apparently random episodes might be held to possess a unity both sufficient and meaningful.[6]

Using Moll's vanity as a point of departure, Starr finds that the book is a straightforward narrative of sin and repentance whose "real coherence seems to lie in the gradual unfolding of inward states, not in the overt action by which they are revealed." [7] This view, while usefully indicating that the book has a potential spiritual structure, ignores Defoe's efforts to impose a coherent pattern on the outward narrative events, disregards the role of necessity rather than vanity in precipitating Moll's actions, and finally, grossly overestimates the degree of

[6] G. A. Starr, *Defoe and Spiritual Autobiography* (Princeton: Princeton University Press, 1965), p. 126.
[7] Ibid., pp. 132–33.

spiritual change which Moll in fact undergoes. Starr accurately points out that the description of religious states in mercantile terms was commonplace rather than shocking to the eighteenth-century mind. He neglects, however, to point out that Moll differs from her more conventional spiritual predecessors in that instead of simply using the language of the marketplace metaphorically to describe her experiences as a Christian, she transmutes the entire Christian experience into a metaphor for her secular existence. In Newgate, for instance, Moll comes closest to voicing traditional Christian sentiments, when she says:

> the views of felicity, the joy, the griefs of life were quite other things; and I had nothing in my thoughts but was so infinitely superiour to what I had known in life, that it appear'd to be the greatest stupidity to lay a weight upon anything, tho' the most valuable in this world.

If Moll were forced to make good her pronouncements, this reflection would carry a good deal of weight. Far more typical, however, is the way in which Jemmy is finally brought to repentance:

> Then I [Moll] let him [Jemmy] know what I had brought over [from Moll's son] in the sloop . . . ; I mean the horses, hogs, and cows, and other stores for our plantation; all which added to his surprize and fill'd his heart with thankfulness; and from this time forward I believe, he was as sincere a penitent, and as thoroughly a reform'd man as ever God's goodness brought back from a profligate, a highwayman and a robber.

Man, in *Moll Flanders,* is most often brought to God by bounty, and the language describing this process forces our attention to focus much more closely on the physical magnificence than on either God's or Jemmy's spiritual attributes. Yet it is precisely those spiritual qualities which are being insisted upon even as our attention is forced away from them. As spiritual autobiographer Moll Flanders is perhaps closer kin to Norman Podhoretz than to the saintly Mr. George Herbert. This relationship, however, is one unrecognized by Moll or, it would seem, by Defoe himself.

On the other hand, the double tension in the book cannot, I think, be satisfactorily explained as a balanced pull of forces which produces a final structural harmony. Howard L. Koonce offers this analysis in his attempt to show how Defoe uses "Moll's muddle" to create a coherent work organized around Defoe's ironic evaluation of his heroine:

> [By] projecting Moll's muddling [into] the incidents of the story, and thereby putting into real conflict the old interests of the criminal narration, Defoe sustained it by means of a similar kind of conflict in the structure of the book. For Moll's consciousness of the structure of the story is at odds with its real form.

Actually, Moll's story is [a] series of episodic variations on the theme of resourcefulness . . . .

In Moll's consciousness, however, her story has all the structure of traditional Christian experience. Her life is to her a kind of journey to salvation . . . . On the structural level, Moll is satisfied that she has . . . changed . . . , that she has worked out a resolution of the conflict within her, her warring impulses come to rest . . . in a . . . state of penitence.

But by setting this apparent movement of the story at odds with the static, non-developing series of episodes, Defoe, in fact, maintained the muddle, and we recognize Moll's resolution to be an absurd . . . logical triumph, in which her sense of morality has been completely absorbed into her sense of destiny.[8]

This assessment seems so compelling that I criticize it with some hesitation. Once again, however, it seems to me to simplify the work itself in the interest of subjecting it to complex analysis. If the surface narrative of *Moll Flanders* were, in fact, as static as Koonce maintains it is, then indeed his view might be the final one. The difficulty is that the narrative in fact moves on the literal level as Moll thinks it does on the spiritual one. Moll may be the same character at the book's end that she was in the beginning, and her principles may remain constant throughout, but at the end of the book she has attained her goal on the realistic level of the primary narrative just as she thinks she has on the Christian level of the implied spiritual narrative. It is not enough to say that she has resolved her internal conflicts by deluding herself about the true nature of her experiences. On the contrary, the true nature of her experiences would seem to make Moll's view of them inevitable. Moll is materially successful; the narrative structure moves upward in a spiral. Thus, Koonce's perceptions of an ironic contrast between literal narrative stagnation and false Christian vision simply do not hold up. If the narrative surface of the book were really static, if, that is, Moll's position in the world were really no more secure at the end than it was at the beginning, then indeed we could say that she was deluding herself about the nature of her fate. But, in fact, it is quite otherwise. At the beginning, Moll is a penniless, dependent orphan, while at the end she is a moneyed, married, propertied lady. While each incident reflects no great change in Moll's conception of herself in relation to her world, the narrative as a whole indicates a consistent movement within the workaday world it creates.

Thus once again we return to the structural difficulties of the book. Crudely put, Defoe's dilemma in *Moll Flanders* has been to find a *modus vivendi* for a poor, solitary girl. The book itself provides evidence for two possible solutions to this problem, the Christian and the

[8] Howard L. Koonce, "Moll's Muddle: Defoe's Use of Irony in *Moll Flanders*," *ELH*, XXX (1963), 384. [See this volume, pp. 49–59.]

secular. In terms of the Christian solution, Moll is made to turn to
God. Having found him, she is no longer alone and the things of this
world no longer have any great significance. This view is the one
voiced by Moll in Newgate and at various other times during the
course of the book. In terms of the secular solution, Moll makes both
money and marriages. Having found these, she is obviously neither
alone nor fearful that the things of this world will escape her. The
narrative structure in terms of which both these solutions are worked
out is superficially similar: both are circular in form—in my beginning
is my end—and spiral in movement. The obvious and unreconciled
question, however, concerns the congruence of the two spirals. There
are roads to both God and Mammon, but neither the gods nor the
roads are necessarily the same.

Defoe, in seeking to combine the two, has been written off as a
bungler or eulogized as an ironist. As usual, the truth lies in the
moderate bog between these extremes. In his attempt to create a work
which would be at once a moral fable and an accurate account of the
realities of a particular life, Defoe creatd a double perspectival structure but failed to provide a sequence of narrative events which would
either develop one point of view in terms of the other or generate a
wider view which could contain the two. The real and the moral are
not yoked to pull together, but are harnessed so that first one pulls and
now the other. First Moll avers that the world is well lost, and then
she sings praises to gaining it. There is nothing in the book—in terms
of style, structure, or characterization—that will allow us to know
whether these two views are meant to be in harmony or in conflict with
each other and, if the latter, with which we are supposed to agree.
Moll's morality is inadequate, solely in structural terms, because her
purported spiritual growth has no consequences in action: even after
her final repentance, when she is in America with Jemmy, Moll remains prudent and secretive as ever. But that, however inadequate,
her morality cannot be meant to be ironically evaluated is equally
apparent because nothing, either in the structure or the characters,
offers the possibility of any other view but Moll's own. Moll, holding
her views, is rewarded, and the logic of events would indicate that we
are meant to be delighted. The structural weakness of the book
results from Defoe's attempts to project a moral meaning upon this
sequence of events. If we are pleased at Moll's worldly success, we
delight in her human vitality, not her morals. If we listen to the moral
statements, we find that the events themselves do not support their
supposed moral weight. The moral structure and the structure of
reality remain divorced because Defoe has failed to coordinate the two
aspects of his narrative purpose. He has created two perspectives
without a narrative adequate to contain both of them. He has not been

able to manipulate reality so that the events themselves create their own moral framework. Because this relationship between the real world and a surrounding moral universe is not completely controlled by Defoe, *Moll Flanders* emerges not as the first English novel, but as a perpetually anomalous and problematic prose fiction.

Chronology of Important Dates

	Defoe	Historical Events
1660	Daniel Defoe [exact date unknown] born in London.	Restoration of Charles II.
1665		68,500 deaths in the Great Plague of London.
Sept. 1666		The Great Fire of London destroyed two-thirds of the city.
1670s	Attended the Rev. James Fisher's school, Dorking, Surrey.	
1674?–79?	Attended the Rev. Charles Morton's academy, Newington Green, Middlesex, to prepare for Presbyterian ministry.	
1678–81		The Popish Plot to restore Roman Catholicism in England.
1683?	Set up in import-export business in Freeman's Yard, Cornhill, London.	
1683	Published 1st political tract (no copy known).	
Jan. 1684	Married Mary Tuffley, said to be daughter of a wine-cooper, with a dowry of £3700.	
Feb. 1685		Charles II succeeded by his Roman Catholic brother, James II.
June 1685	Joined Protestant Duke of Monmouth's rebellion in Somersetshire.	

1685–92	Travelled frequently throughout England and the continent on business.	
Jan. 1688	Admitted to the Butcher's Company, a trade guild.	
1688	Published first extant political tract against James II.	
Nov.–Dec. 1688		William, Prince of Orange, landed at Torbay, Devonshire. James II fled London. Louis XIV declared war on England.
Dec. 1688	Rode to Henley to join advancing forces of William.	
1692	Wartime losses of shipping which Defoe had insured forced him into bankruptcy for £17,-000.	
Sept. 1697		Treaty of Ryswick concluded between France and England.
Jan. 1701	Published *The True-Born Englishman* in defense of William III.	
May 1701	Presented *Legion's Memorial* to Robert Harley, Speaker of the House of Commons.	
Dec. 1701	Youngest child, Sophia, baptized.	
March 1702		William III succeeded by Queen Anne.
May 1702		England declared war on France over Spanish Succession.
1703	Arrested for publishing a seditious libel, *The Shortest Way with the Dissenters* (1702), attacking the Church of England for persecuting dissenters. Imprisoned, heavily fined, and exposed in the pillory.	

Nov. 1703	Released from Newgate prison by Robert Harley, for whom Defoe undertook propaganda and intelligence work until 1714.	
Feb. 1704– June 1713	Wrote the *Review,* a biweekly journal of opinion.	
Aug. 1704		Marlborough's victory over the French at Blenheim, in Bavaria.
1706–10	Frequently in Scotland.	
May 1706		Marlborough's victory at Ramillies, in Brabant.
March 1707		Act of Union between Scotland and England.
ca. Jan. 1708	Moved to Stoke Newington, suburb north of London, where he lived the rest of his life.	
July 1708		Marlborough's victory at Oudenarde, in Flanders.
1713	Repeatedly arrested by Harley's political enemies, once for publishing *And what if the Pretender should come?* and two more ironical tracts in support of the Hanoverian Succession.	
Aug. 1714		Fall of Harley ministry. Queen Anne succeeded by George I, of Hanover.
March 1715	Published *The Family Instructor,* first didactic treatise.	
1715–30	Undertook propaganda and intelligence work for successive Whig ministries.	
April 25, 1719	Published *The Life and Strange Surprizing Adventures of Robinson Crusoe of York, Mariner.*	

June 1720   Published *The Life, Adventures, and Pyracies of the Famous Captain Singleton.*

Jan. 1722   Published *The Fortunes and Misfortunes of the Famous Moll Flanders.*

March 1722   Published *A Journal of the Plague Year.*

Dec. 1722   Published *The History and Remarkable Life of the Truly Honourable Col. Jacque.*

Feb. 1724   Published *The Fortunate Mistress: Or . . . Roxana.*

June 1727   George I succeeded by George II.

April 24, 1731   Died in Ropemaker's Alley, hiding from creditors.

Notes on the Editor and Contributors

ROBERT C. ELLIOTT is Professor of English Literature and Chairman of the Department of Literature at the University of California, San Diego. He is the author of *The Power of Satire* and *The Shape of Utopia.*

ROBERT ALTER is Associate Professor of Hebrew and Comparative Literature at the University of California, Berkeley. He is the author of *Fielding and the Nature of the Novel.*

LEE EDWARDS is Assistant Professor of English at the University of Massachusetts in Amherst.

HOWARD L. KOONCE is Assistant Professor of English at Colby College.

MAXIMILLIAN E. NOVAK teaches English at the University of California, Los Angeles. He is the author of numerous studies of Defoe.

CESARE PAVESE was a brilliant Italian writer and critic of American literature.

G. A. STARR teaches English at the University of California, Berkeley; he is the author of *Defoe and Spiritual Autobiography.*

DOROTHY VAN GHENT wrote *The English Novel: Form and Function.*

IAN WATT is Professor of English at Stanford. He has recently edited a volume on *The Augustan Age.*

REED WHITTEMORE, poet and critic, is Professor of English at the National Institute of Public Affairs.

VIRGINIA WOOLF is the famous novelist and critic.

Selected Bibliography

See the works cited in the Introduction to this volume.

Biography

Sutherland, James. *Defoe*. London, 1937. A perceptive and readable life, although recent researches have made it somewhat out of date. Sutherland has also a 36-page pamphlet in the Writers and Their Work series: *Defoe*. London, 1954; reprinted 1965.

Moore, John R. *Daniel Defoe: Citizen of the Modern World*. Chicago, 1958. Detailed biography by an eminent Defoe scholar.

Interpretations

Martin, Terence. "The Unity of *Moll Flanders*." *MLQ*, 22 (1961), 115–24. A study of cyclical repetition in the plot elements of *Moll Flanders*.

Novak, Maximillian E. "Moll Flanders' First Love." *Papers of the Michigan Academy of Science, Arts and Letters*, 46 (1961), 635–43. Defoe's use of irony in the account of Moll's downfall.

Donoghue, Denis. "The Values of *Moll Flanders*." *Sewanee Review*, 71 (1963), 287–303. "Moll cannot be said to have a character at all."

Columbus, Robert R. "Conscious Artistry in *Moll Flanders*." *SEL*, 3 (1963), 415–32. A study of point of view in the novel.

Price, Martin. *To the Palace of Wisdom*. New York, 1964, pp. 263–75. Excellent commentary on Defoe's artistry.

Donovan, Robert Alan. "The Two Heroines of *Moll Flanders*." In *The Shaping Vision*, pp. 21–46. Ithaca, New York, 1966. Stylistic study of *Moll* as a work of irony.

Brooks, Douglas. "*Moll Flanders*." *Essays in Criticism*, 19 (1969), 46–59. Patterns of repetition and cross-reference in the plot of *Moll Flanders*.

TWENTIETH CENTURY
INTERPRETATIONS

MAYNARD MACK, *Series Editor*
Yale University

NOW AVAILABLE
Collections of Critical Essays
ON

ADVENTURES OF HUCKLEBERRY FINN
ALL FOR LOVE
THE AMBASSADORS
ARROWSMITH
AS YOU LIKE IT
BLEAK HOUSE
THE BOOK OF JOB
THE CASTLE
CORIOLANUS
DOCTOR FAUSTUS
DON JUAN
DUBLINERS
THE DUCHESS OF MALFI
ENDGAME
EURIPIDES' ALCESTIS
THE FALL OF THE HOUSE OF USHER
A FAREWELL TO ARMS
THE FROGS
GRAY'S ELEGY
THE GREAT GATSBY
GULLIVER'S TRAVELS
HAMLET
HARD TIMES
HENRY IV, PART TWO
HENRY V
THE ICEMAN COMETH
JULIUS CAESAR

(continued on next page)

(*continued from previous page*)

KEATS'S ODES
LIGHT IN AUGUST
LORD JIM
MAJOR BARBARA
MEASURE FOR MEASURE
THE MERCHANT OF VENICE
MUCH ADO ABOUT NOTHING
THE NIGGER OF THE "NARCISSUS"
OEDIPUS REX
THE OLD MAN AND THE SEA
PAMELA
THE PLAYBOY OF THE WESTERN WORLD
THE PORTRAIT OF A LADY
A PORTRAIT OF THE ARTIST AS A YOUNG MAN
THE PRAISE OF FOLLY
PRIDE AND PREJUDICE
THE RAPE OF THE LOCK
THE RIME OF THE ANCIENT MARINER
ROBINSON CRUSOE
ROMEO AND JULIET
SAMSON AGONISTES
THE SCARLET LETTER
SIR GAWAIN AND THE GREEN KNIGHT
SONGS OF INNOCENCE AND OF EXPERIENCE
SONS AND LOVERS
THE SOUND AND THE FURY
THE TEMPEST
TESS OF THE D'URBERVILLES
TOM JONES
TWELFTH NIGHT
UTOPIA
VANITY FAIR
WALDEN
THE WASTE LAND
WOMEN IN LOVE
WUTHERING HEIGHTS

TWENTIETH CENTURY VIEWS

British Authors